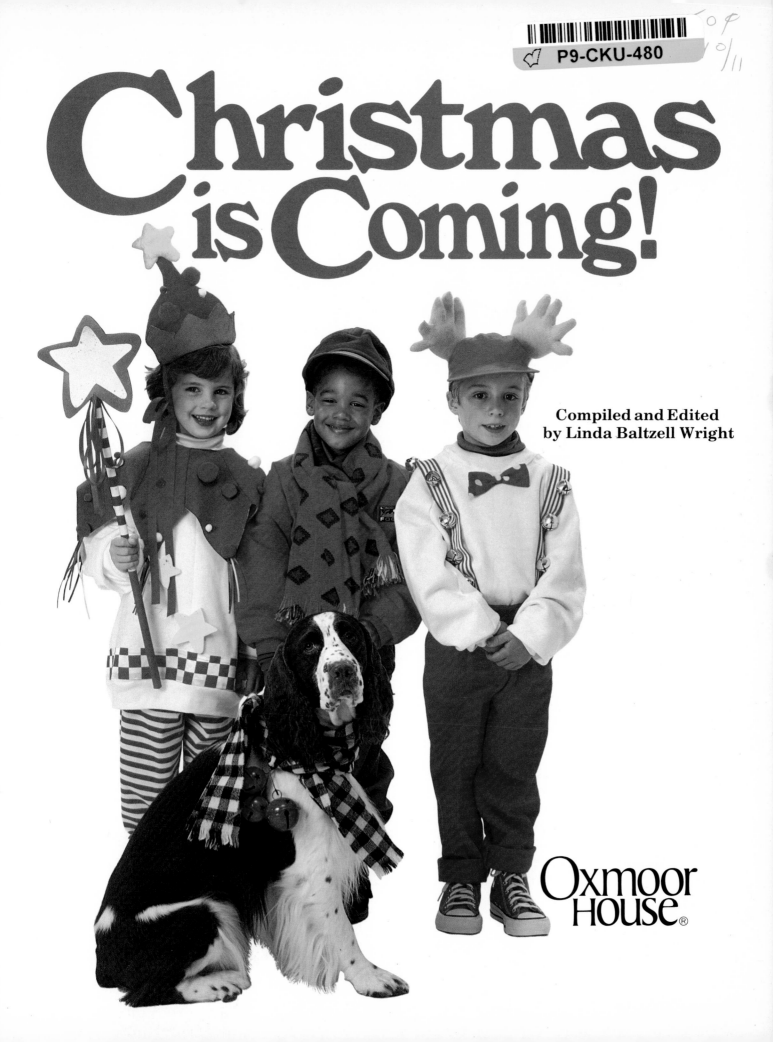

Christmas is Coming!

Compiled and Edited
by Linda Baltzell Wright

Oxmoor House®

Contents

A Visit to the North Pole

©1992 by Oxmoor House, Inc.
Book Division of Southern Progress Corporation
P.O. Box 2463, Birmingham, Alabama 35201

Library of Congress Catalog Card Number: 84-63030
ISBN: 0-8487-1110-6
ISSN: 0883-9077
Manufactured in the United States of America
First Printing

Editor-in-Chief: Nancy J. Fitzpatrick
Director of Manufacturing: Jerry Higdon
Art Director: James Boone
Copy Chief: Mary Jean Haddin

Christmas is Coming!

Editor: Linda Baltzell Wright
Assistant Editor: Lelia Gray Neil
Illustrator and Designer: Barbara Ball
Editorial Assistant: Shannon Leigh Sexton
Assistant Copy Editor: Susan Smith Cheatham
Senior Photographer: John O'Hagan
Photostylist: Connie Formby
Production Manager: Rick Litton
Associate Production Manager: Theresa L. Beste
Production Assistant: Pam Beasley Bullock

Children's Workshop: Happy Holiday Crafts

Parents' Workshop: Great Gifts for Children

Designers & Contributors

A Word to Parents

As busy parents, what do we need more of? Time with our children, time to make memories. And at Christmastime this seems especially important. *Christmas is Coming!* can't give you more time, but we can give you lots of ideas for making your holidays memorable. Cuddle up with the kids to read the poem, "Searching for Santa." Then let them help photocopy their own North Pole Village to color, cut, and glue. (Feel free to photocopy the designs for your personal use.)

Keep those crayons, scissors, and glue handy, because in "Children's Workshop," the kids will discover all kinds of ideas for making holiday decorations and presents. There's a Christmas tree banner to sponge-paint, pop-up package toppers to cut out, and silly pins to glue.

Before your child begins any of the projects, however, we suggest that you look over the instructions. At a quick glance, you'll see that the projects are rated for difficulty with a Level 1, 2, or 3. Also check the "you will need" list. If "a grown-up" is listed, you will know that we recommend that you help with one or more steps in the project.

When you are allowed a break, explore "Parents' Workshop." You'll find adorable clothes and toys that will delight your child. You don't have to be an expert sewer or sawer to find just the right gift to make.

With *Christmas is Coming!* in hand, start your memory making today. Gather your supplies, add a pinch of childish exuberance, and you and your family are sure to have a holiday to remember.

A Visit to the North Pole

Searching for Santa

Twas the day before Christmas
and rainy and cold.
I was thinking of presents
that Santa's bag might hold.

So with my Christmas list in hand
I thought I'd take a chance
and begin my Santa search,
hoping to catch a glance.

Where to start exploring
became very clear:
He'd be at the North Pole
this time of the year.

A magic red sleigh
carried me in flight
with never a stop
until land was in sight.

8

Welcoming me there
wasn't Santa himself.
But standing in for him
was a small, funny elf.

I asked him, "Where's St. Nick?"
But he just shyly smiled.
Then he whispered, "Here's a
map with a clue every mile."

Unrolling the map
  I found the first clue.
  This was going to be fun—
    I'd see Santa, I knew!

Said the clue, "Santa with his
    sweet tooth
needs a lot of sweets.
That's why we have a forest
filled with Lollipop Tree treats."

I searched through the forest
where lollipops abound,
but, alas, St. Nicholas
was not to be found.

I was looking for the next clue
when a reindeer appeared.
"Read it out loud," he said,
"so we can both hear."

So I read the second clue:
"The Post Office is a hub
of sacks full of letters
from St. Nick's fan club."

"Yes, that must be the place,"
the tall reindeer said.
"We'll catch Santa answering
the letters he's read."

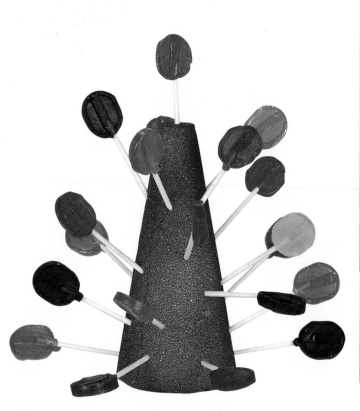

We saw deer who were stamping
letters by the pound,
but, alas, St. Nicholas
was not to be found.

Then on to the next stop.
The clue said, "Quickly steal
to the place where toy soldiers
and dolls become real."

"At the Whistle While You Work
  Shoppe,
Santa likes to play
with toys the elves are making
for gifts on Christmas Day."

12

The elves were working swiftly,
hammering up and down,
but, alas, St. Nicholas
was not to be found.

The fourth clue said, "Follow
the nose on your face.
The source of scents delicious
will lead you to the place."

We followed our noses
to the Eats & Treats Deli.
We were sure to find Santa
getting food for his belly.

Plates full of sandwiches
and floats did abound,
but, alas, St. Nicholas
was not to be found.

"Where wind and snow are
measured"
our next clue said to go.
He'd need a weather forecast
so his sleigh could land, you know.

Windmills turning briskly
mean a cold and blustery night.
Santa's sure to check the Weather
  Station
before making his long flight.

Well, we looked high and low
from the sky to the ground,
but, alas, St. Nicholas
was not to be found.

To the last clue on the map
we gave special attention.
"Who flies Santa's sleigh?"
Eight names we could mention.

19

Aha! At last. He can't go far
without his trusty deer.
To the Deer Dorm we'd go
and in each bed we'd peer.

In the dark of the night, all the
beds were lined up straight.
But not one reindeer could we find.
Oh dear! Were we too late?

With all our hopes dashed
we turned at last to go,
but we heard someone whistle and
call over the snow.

"Hurry home!" he exclaimed
as he drove out of sight.
   "Happy Christmas to all
   and to all a good night."

The moon in the night sky
on this Christmas Eve
gave to all who could see
a clear path to believe.

The North Pole Village

After you've traveled around the North Pole with the explorer, reindeer, and elf, you can go on to invent new adventures for yourself! Decide which of the buildings pictured here you would like to make. Have a grown-up photocopy the patterns for you at full-size to make the village. Or, to make the ornaments, ask the grown-up to make the patterns smaller by reducing them on the photocopy machine.

North Pole Entrance

You will need:
A grown-up
Heavyweight white paper
Colored markers
Scissors
Glue

1. For the entrance to the North Pole, **ask the grown-up** to photocopy the patterns for the arch and supports onto the heavyweight paper. Color the pieces and cut them out.

2. Glue the top edge of the North Pole sign to the middle of the arch.

3. Fold 1 support where marked. Glue the tab to the back of the arch base, lining up the bottom of the support and the bottom of the arch. Repeat for the other support. Let them dry.

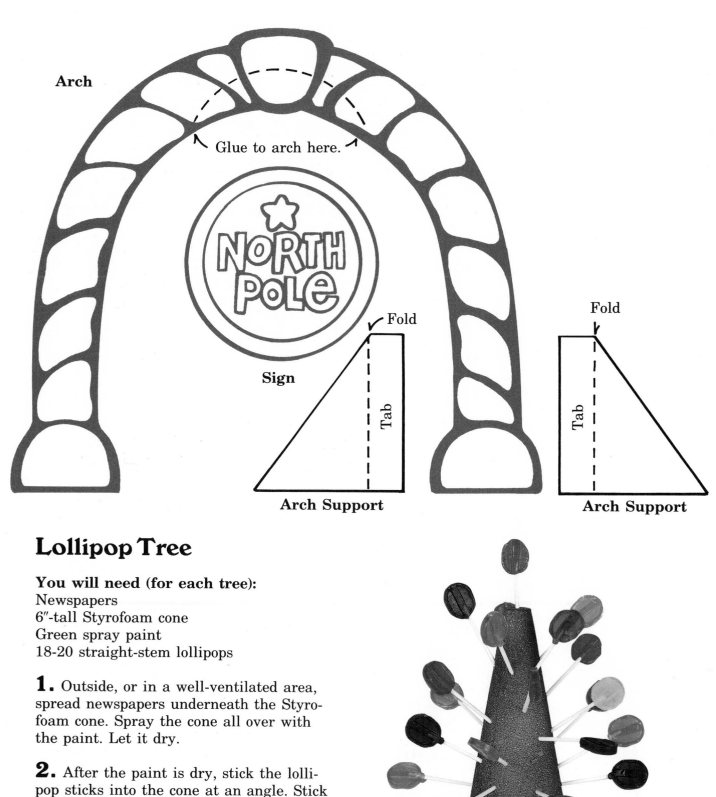

Arch

Glue to arch here.

North Pole

Sign

Fold

Tab

Arch Support

Fold

Tab

Arch Support

Lollipop Tree

You will need (for each tree):
Newspapers
6″-tall Styrofoam cone
Green spray paint
18-20 straight-stem lollipops

1. Outside, or in a well-ventilated area, spread newspapers underneath the Styrofoam cone. Spray the cone all over with the paint. Let it dry.

2. After the paint is dry, stick the lollipop sticks into the cone at an angle. Stick them in deep enough so they don't wiggle.

North Pole Village Buildings

You will need (for each building):
A grown-up
Heavyweight white paper
Colored markers
Scissors
Glue stick

For the post office:
White paper
Toothpick

For the ornaments:
Large-eyed needle
10″ of heavy thread

Making the Buildings

1. Ask the grown-up to photocopy the pattern for each building you want 2 times onto the heavyweight paper.

2. Color both copies with the markers and cut them out. Cut off Tab A on 1 of the copies.

3. Fold the building along all the broken lines. Fold all the tabs to the inside and glue the 2 building pieces together.

4. **For the post office flag:** Color both patterns and cut them out. Glue the tab around the toothpick. Glue the backs of the flags together, covering the tab. Stick the toothpick into the X over the front door of the post office.

5. **For the weather station:** Fold all the tabs to the inside and glue the 2 building pieces together. For the observation deck, color the pieces and cut them out. Fold 1 piece along fold line A. Then fold the piece toward the back along fold line B. Then fold it forward along fold line C. Repeat for the other piece. Fold in

Level 2

the tab on 1 piece and glue the 2 pieces together along 1 end. Apply glue to the back of the area below fold line C and glue the deck to the weather station along the placement lines. Fold under the remaining tab and glue in place.

Making the Ornaments

1. **Ask the grown-up** to photocopy the buildings you want 2 times at 60% onto the heavyweight paper.

2. To assemble the ornament, repeat steps 2-5 of Making the Buildings.

3. To hang the ornament, thread the needle and insert it through 1 side of the roof, about ¼″ from the top edge of the building. Push the needle all the way through to the other side. Take off the needle and tie the ends of the thread in a knot.

Post Office Flag

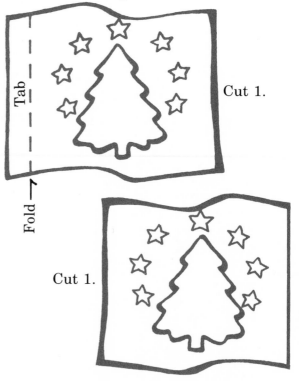

Tab

Fold →

Cut 1.

Cut 1.

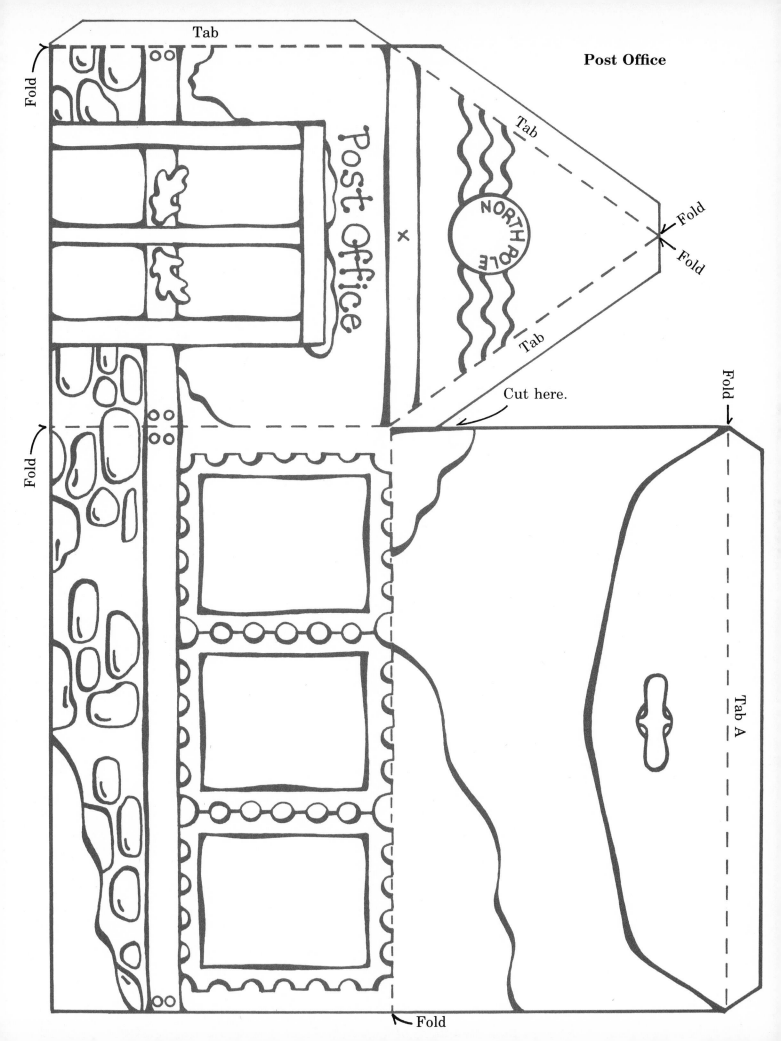

Post Office

Tab

Fold

Fold

Post Office

Tab

Tab

NORTH POLE

Fold

Fold

Cut here.

Fold

Fold

Tab A

Fold

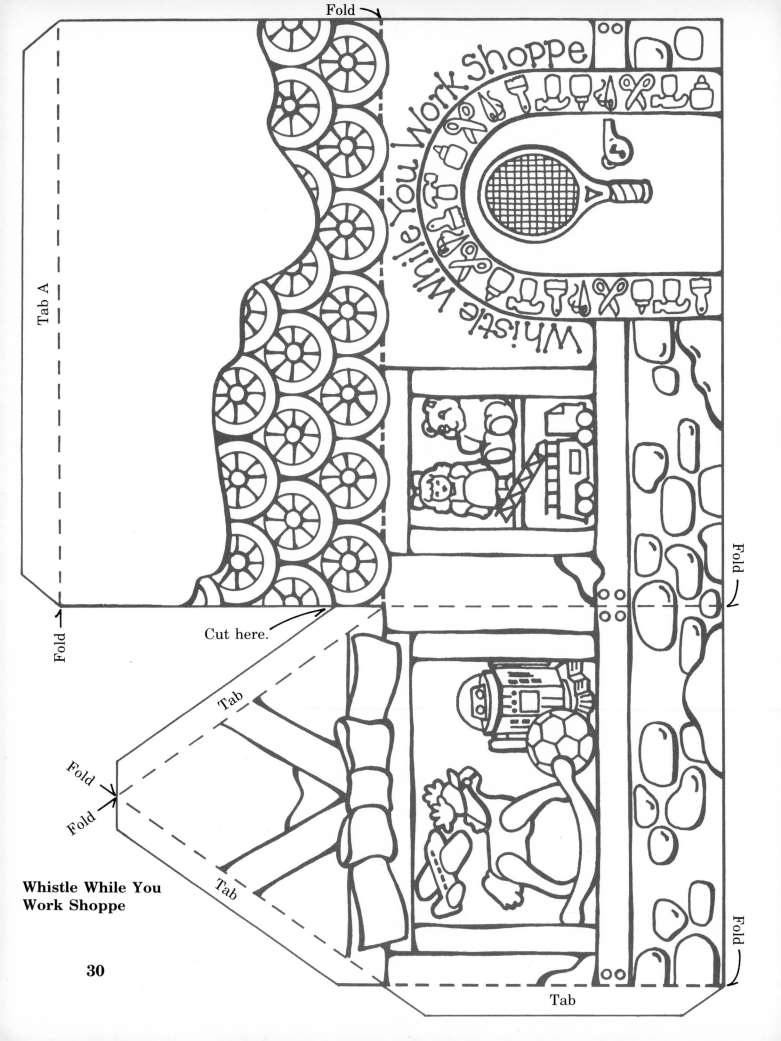

Fold

Tab A

Fold

Cut here.

Whistle While You Work Shoppe

Fold

Fold

Tab

Tab

**Whistle While You
Work Shoppe**

30

Fold

Fold

Fold

Tab

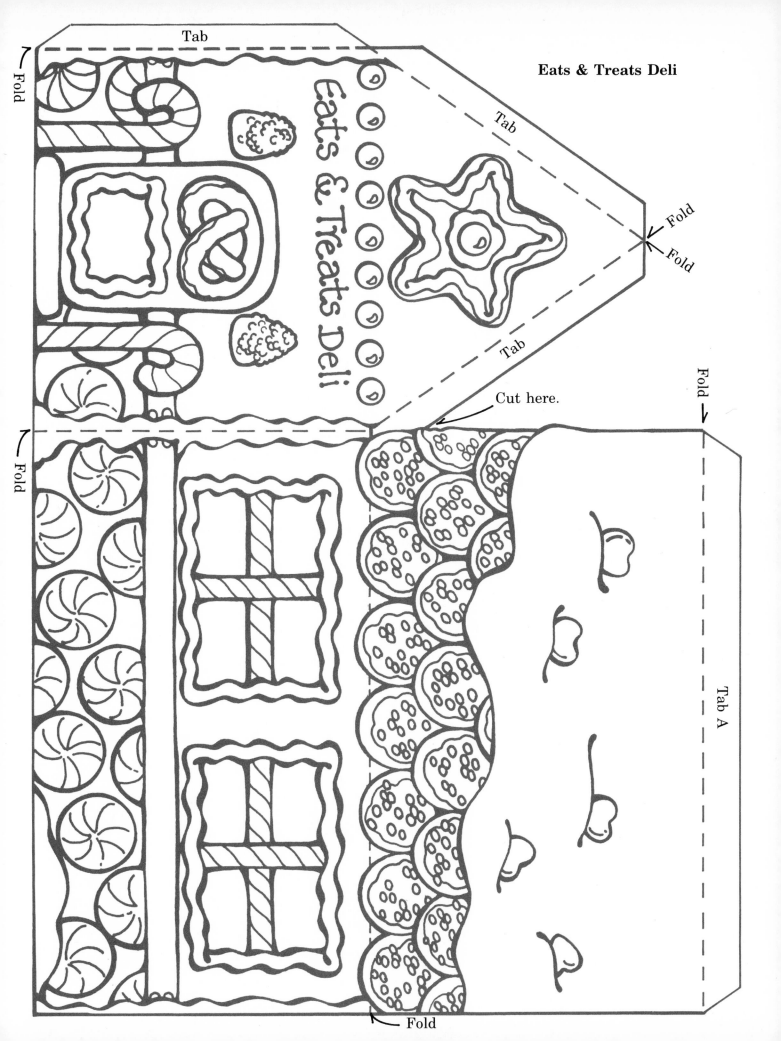

Tab

Fold

Eats & Treats Deli

Tab

Fold

Fold

Fold

Tab

Cut here.

Fold

Fold

Fold

Tab A

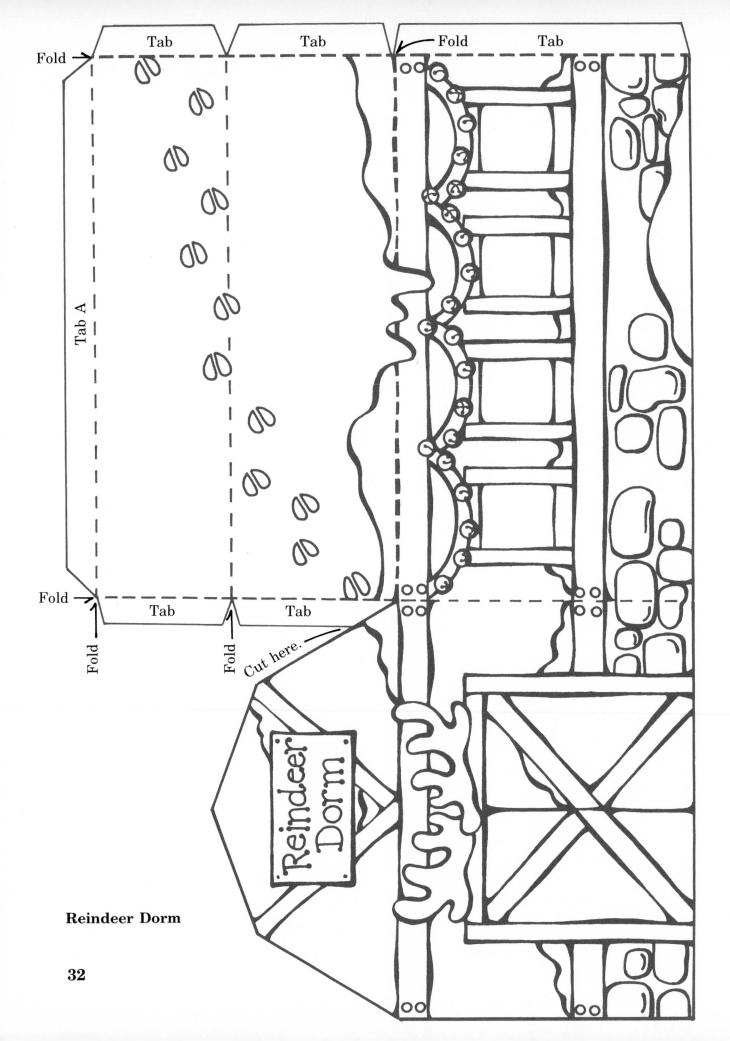

Reindeer Dorm

32

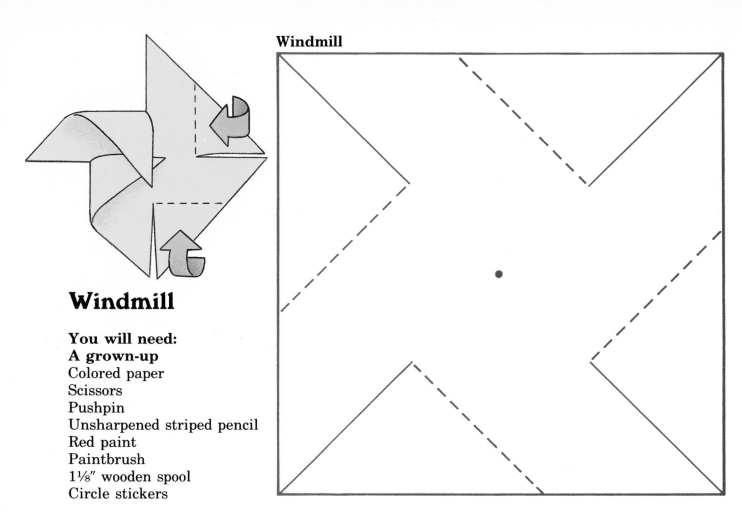

Windmill

You will need:
A grown-up
Colored paper
Scissors
Pushpin
Unsharpened striped pencil
Red paint
Paintbrush
1⅛″ wooden spool
Circle stickers

Note to parents: Be careful not to let little fingers get pricked with the pushpin.

1. **Ask the grown-up** to photocopy the pattern onto the colored paper. Cut out the windmill, cutting along all solid lines.

2. Fold on all broken lines so that the points overlap at the center mark. Do not crease the fold lines.

3. Hold the points in the center and stick the pushpin through them. Then push the end of the pin into the side of the pencil eraser.

4. Paint the spool red. Put it aside to dry.

5. Decorate the end of the pushpin with the stickers.

6. Stand the windmill in the spool.

Level 2

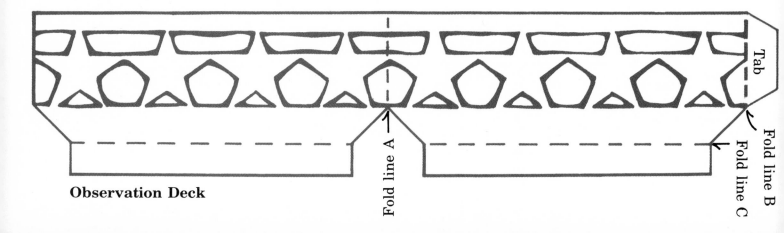

Observation Deck

Paper Dolls

These cute paper dolls with all of their outfits can take on any role. But whatever they're doing, they'll be dressed for the North Pole!

You will need:
A grown-up
Heavyweight white paper
White paper
Colored markers
Scissors
Tracing paper

1. Ask the grown-up to photocopy the Explorer, Reindeer, and Elf and their stands onto the heavyweight paper. Photocopy the clothes onto the other paper.

2. Color the paper dolls and their outfits with the markers. Cut them out. Be sure you don't cut the tabs off the clothes.

3. To put the clothes on the paper dolls, lay the clothes on the dolls and fold the tabs to the back.

4. To make the dolls stand up, cut a slit between the doll's feet. Cut out the stand and cut the slit where marked. Insert the doll's feet into the slit in the stand. Line up the bottom of the feet and the bottom of the stand.

Doll Stand

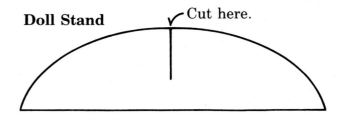

Cut here.

Explorer

Explorer's Uniform

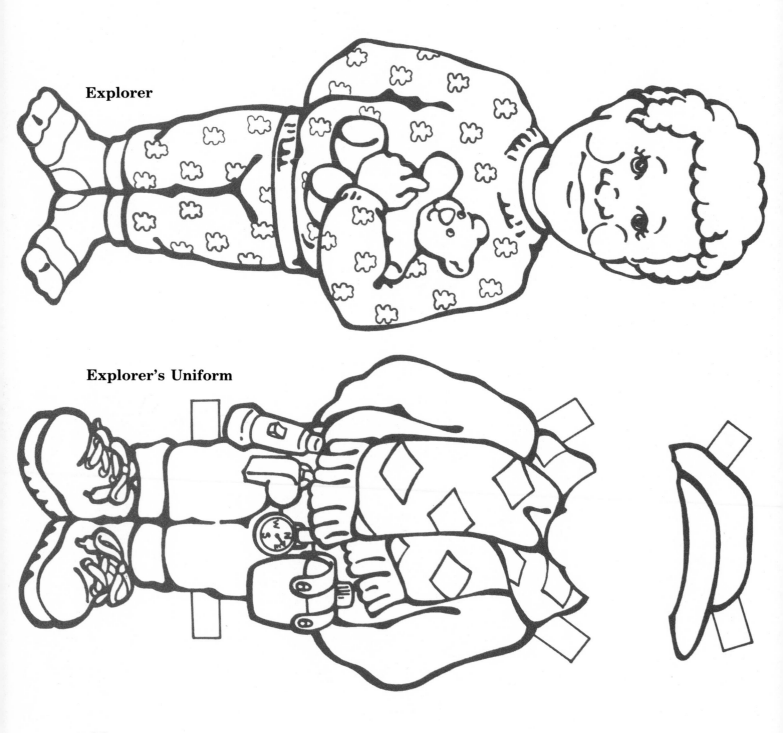

Elf

Official Uniform

Doll Stand ✓ Cut here.

Toymaker's Uniform

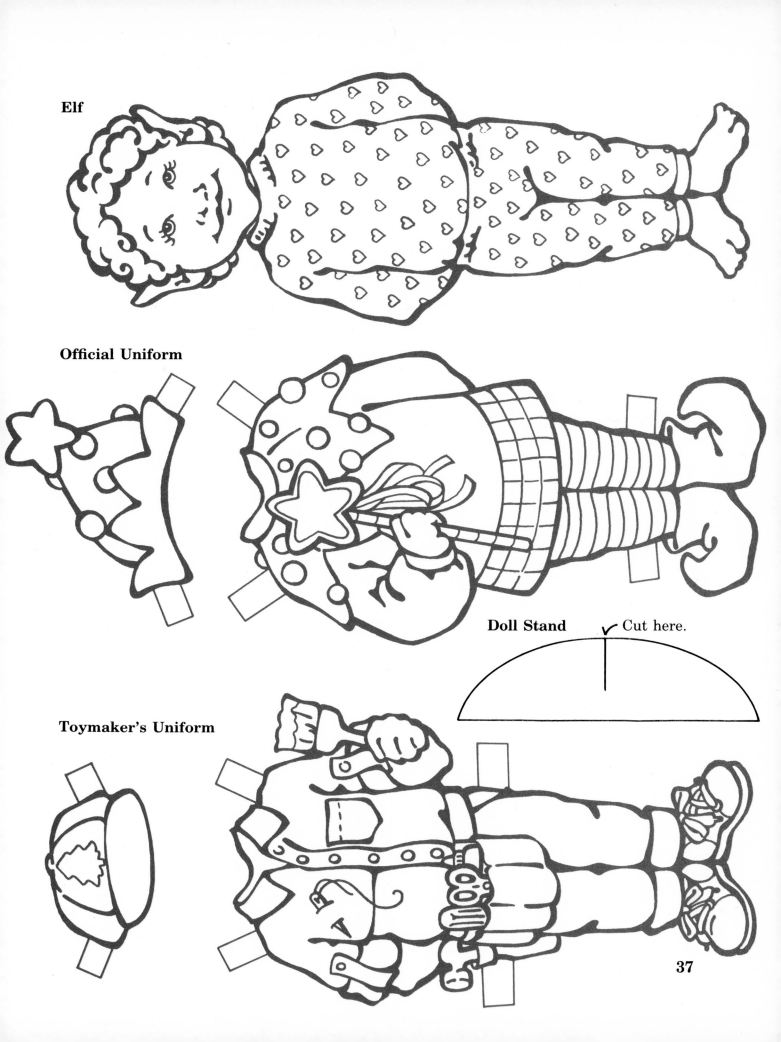

37

Reindeer

Doll Stand ⌄Cut here.

Official Uniform

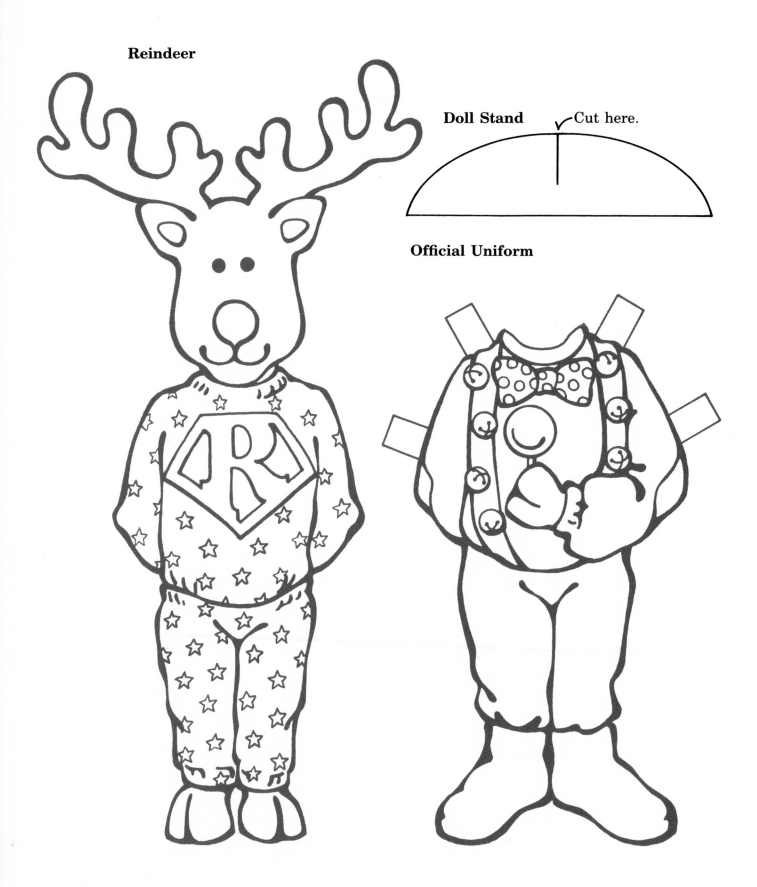

38

Chef's Uniform

Postal Worker's Uniform

Children's Workshop
Happy Holiday Crafts

Christmas Tree Banner

Even your house can say, "Christmas is coming!" Hang this banner on your front porch, and everyone will see the spirit of Christmas stamped all over it.

You will need:

Tracing paper
Pencil
Newspaper
1 yard (45"-wide) white weatherproof
   nylon fabric
Yardstick
Fabric glue
4½ yards (⅝"-wide) green grosgrain
   ribbon
4½ yards (1½"-wide) red grosgrain ribbon
Scissors
Liquid ravel preventer
Pop-up sponge (6" x 6" x 1¾")
Acrylic paint: green, red
2 paper plates
1 yard (⅝"-diameter) plastic tubing
2 yards (½"-diameter) white rope
2 (1½") red wooden beads with ½" holes

1. Trace and transfer the patterns.

2. Cover the area where you are going
to work with newspaper.

3. Fold under ½" on each edge of the
nylon fabric and glue it in place. On 2
sides and 1 end, fold under another ½".
Glue them in place. Fold the other end
under 2½". Glue just the edge of the first
fold to the back of the nylon to make a

casing for the plastic tubing. Insert the yardstick through the casing. This will keep the glue from seeping through.

4. Measure and cut 2 pieces of green ribbon to fit across the top and bottom of the banner. Apply liquid ravel preventer to the ribbon ends. Glue the ribbon across the top and across the bottom edge of the banner. Measure and cut 2 pieces of green ribbon for the sides of the banner. Apply liquid ravel preventer to the ribbon ends. Glue the ribbon in place.

Repeat these steps with the red ribbon, placing the red ribbon edges just inside the green ribbon edges. Let the glue dry. Remove the yardstick from the casing.

5. Trace the patterns onto the sponge and cut them out. Wet the sponge shapes and squeeze out the excess water.

6. To make the tree, pour green paint onto a paper plate. Dip the child-shaped sponge into the paint. (Practice stamping your sponge on paper a few times before you begin the banner.) Begin stamping on the banner 2″ from the left ribbon edge and 6″ from the bottom ribbon edge. Make a row of 8 children, placing the children

½″ apart. Make the next row with 7 children, each standing on the shoulders of the children in the first row. Continue until there is just 1 child at the top. Let the paint dry.

7. Press the tree-trunk-shaped sponge in the green paint and center it underneath the tree. Stamp the trunk. Let the paint dry.

8. Pour the red paint onto a paper plate. Press the heart-shaped sponge into the paint and press a heart between the arms of all the children to connect them. Continue stamping hearts until all of the arms are joined.

9. To make the tree stand, stamp 1 row of 5 hearts right below the tree trunk. Then stamp 3 rows of 4 hearts each beneath the first row (see photo). Let the paint dry.

45

Heart

Child

Tree Trunk

10. To hang the banner, insert the plastic tube through the casing. String the rope through the tube. String 1 bead on each end of the rope, and knot the ends of the rope.

Origami Ornaments

Using the art of Japanese paper folding, you can turn plain paper into holiday shapes. And the simple folds of the slick paper will catch the light when hung from your tree.

Note: This project may be made with any paper. However, origami paper is easy to fold. It comes in squares and is colored on 1 side. If you don't use origami paper, check to be sure your paper is square by folding the paper in half diagonally. The edges should line up perfectly. Trim them if necessary. Work on a solid surface. Make all creases crisp by running a ruler or your fingernail along the edge.

Star

You will need (for 1 star):
1 (5″-square) yellow origami paper
Hole punch
6″ piece of paper ribbon

1. Place the paper in front of you. With the right side facing up, fold on the diagonal lines as shown in the diagram. Open the paper and lay it flat.

2. Turn the paper over with the wrong side facing up. Fold the paper in half vertically. Then open the paper and fold it again horizontally. Open the paper and lay it flat.

3. With the wrong side facing up, fold 2 opposite corners to the center as shown.

4. Fold 1 side corner toward the center as shown in the diagram. Do the same thing with the other 3 sides.

5. Turn the paper right side up and crease on the fold lines.

6. With the hole punch, make a hole at the top of the star. For a hanger, run the ribbon through the hole and tie it in a knot.

Christmas Tree

You will need (for 1 tree):
1 (5″-square) green origami paper
Hole punch
6″ piece of paper ribbon

1. Place the paper in front of you. With the wrong side facing up, fold on the diagonal. Open the paper and lay it flat.

2. Fold opposite corners to the center crease as shown in the diagram.

3. Now, fold the final corner up.

4. Unfold only this last fold, and fold the paper in half along the center diagonal crease.

5. Make a new crease by folding the bottom point to the left corner as shown; then unfold. Fold again along the same line, but this time fold it to the back. Then unfold.

6. To make your last fold, fold the bottom point as shown in the diagram. Unfold and fold again along the same line to the back. Then unfold.

7. Open the tree with the right side facing you. To form the base of the trunk, fold the paper to the back at the last crease you made. Pinch the center fold in the trunk and the other folds.

8. With the hole punch, make a hole at the top of the tree. For a hanger, run the ribbon through the hole and tie in a knot.

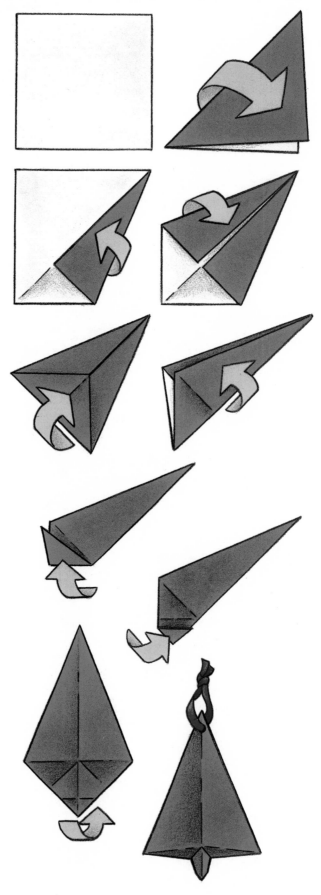

49

Candy  Cane Mice

Twas the night before Christmas, and hung on the tree, were green felt mice just as cute as could be! With some felt, wiggle eyes, and glue, you can make a mouse or two!

You will need (for 1 mouse):
Tracing paper
Pencil
Scissors
Felt: green, red
Fabric glue
Red pom-pom
Wiggle eyes
Candy cane

1. Trace and transfer the patterns and markings.

2. From the green felt, cut 1 body and 2 ears. From the red felt, cut 2 inner ears. Cut slits in the body as marked on the pattern.

3. Center and glue 1 red inner ear on 1 ear. Repeat for the other ear. Glue the wiggle eyes and the pom-pom nose to the body.

4. With the red side up, slide the thin end of 1 ear through 1 ear slit. Do the same with the other ear. Turn the mouse over and glue the end of each ear to the back of the mouse.

5. Slide a candy cane through the candy cane slits on the body.

Body

Ear Slit

Candy Cane Slit

Candy Cane Slit

Ear Slit

Ear

Inner Ear

Clothespin Angels

A host of heavenly angels can float from tree branches, mantels, or packages. Simple and sparkling, these winged ornaments will make everybody smile.

You will need (for 1 angel):
Tracing paper
Pencil
Scissors
Glue
7" (2¾"-wide) crinkle-foil ribbon
2¾" x 7" piece of posterboard
Clothespin
Scrap of gold tinsel
1 pair of 4mm wiggle eyes
Fine-point red marker

1. Trace and cut out the pattern for the wings.

2. Glue the ribbon, right side up, to the posterboard. Let it dry.

3. Place the wing pattern on the poster-board and trace around it. Cut out the wings.

4. On the ribbon side of the wings, put a line of glue down the center. Open the clothespin and slip the wings inside it, closing the clothespin on the glue. Let the glue dry.

5. Glue the piece of tinsel to the top of the clothespin for the halo. Let it dry.

6. Glue the wiggle eyes to the clothespin below the halo. Draw a mouth below the eyes with the red marker.

Wings
Cut 1.

Santa & Reindeer  Wraps

Recycling has never looked so cute! When you transform empty stationery boxes into jolly Christmas wraps, you may have to convince friends that Santa and the reindeer aren't really the presents— the presents are inside.

Santa Wrap

You will need:
Pink tissue paper
Stationery box with transparent lid
Tracing paper
Pencil
Scissors
Green posterboard
Construction paper: white, red, black
Founder's Adhesive glue

1. With the pink tissue paper, wrap a gift that will fit inside box. Put the gift in the box and spread out the paper to fill up the box.

2. Trace and cut out the patterns.

3. From the green posterboard, cut 1 beard, 1 hat, and 1 mustache. From the white paper, cut 1 inner beard, 1 inner mustache, 1 hat trim, and 1 pom-pom. From the red paper, cut 1 inner hat and 1 nose. From the black paper, cut 2 eyes.

4. With the Founder's Adhesive, glue the eyes to the center of the box lid. Glue the nose just below the eyes. Glue the inner white mustache to the green mustache. Glue the mustache below the nose so that the mustache extends below the lower edge of the box lid.

5. Center and glue the white inner beard to the green beard.

6. To assemble the hat, center and glue the inner red hat to the green hat. Glue the hat trim and the pom-pom on the hat.

7. Glue the bottom of the box to the white beard.

8. Glue the hat to the box lid. Let dry.

55

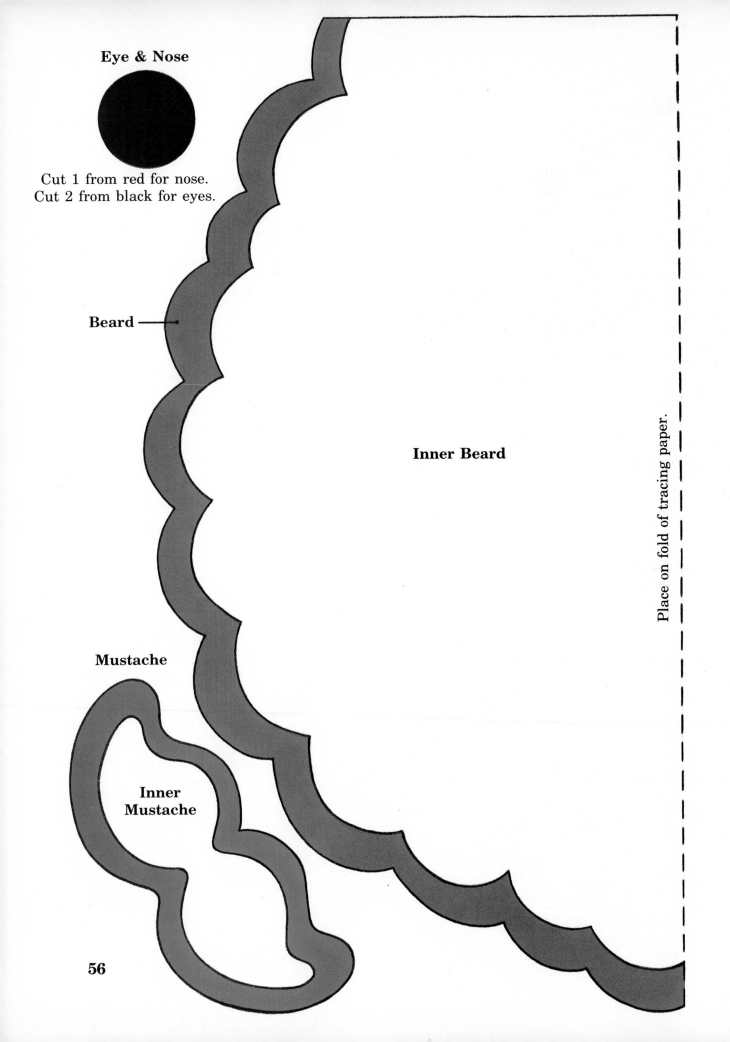

Eye & Nose

Cut 1 from red for nose.
Cut 2 from black for eyes.

Beard

Inner Beard

Mustache

Inner Mustache

Place on fold of tracing paper.

56

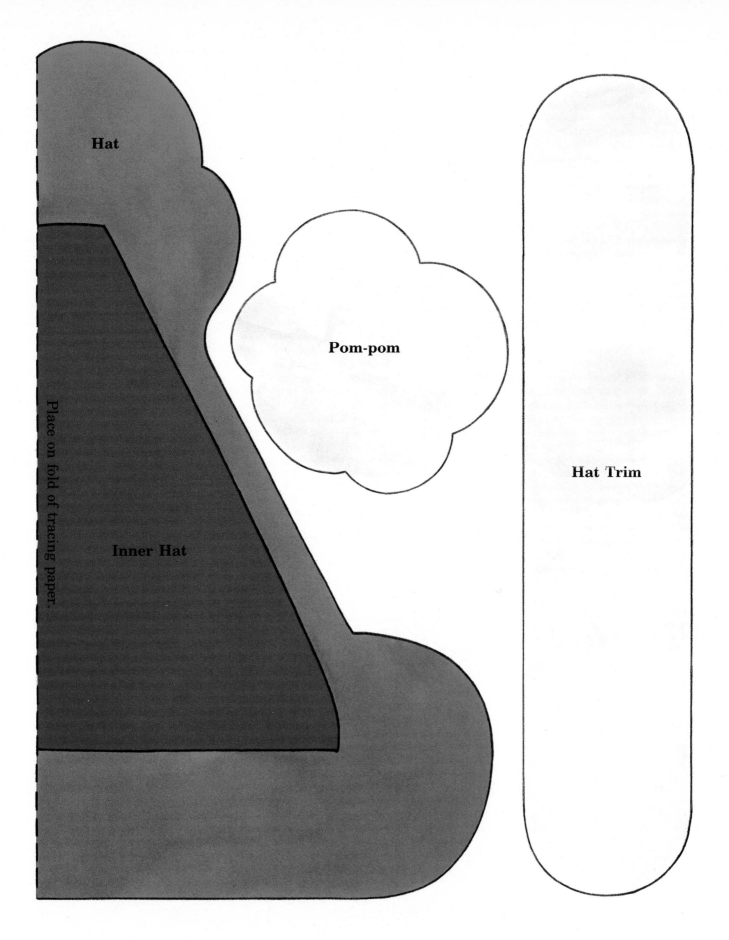

Hat

Place on fold of tracing paper.

Inner Hat

Pom-pom

Hat Trim

Reindeer Wrap

You will need:
Brown paper from grocery sacks
Stationery box with transparent lid
Tracing paper
Red posterboard
Pencil
Scissors
Construction paper: red, yellow, green,
    black
Founder's Adhesive glue
Red tissue paper with white dots
Curling paper ribbon

1. With the brown paper, wrap a gift that fits in the box. Put the gift in the box and spread out the paper to fill the box.

2. Trace and cut out the patterns.

3. From the red posterboard, cut 2 antlers, 1 head, and 1 tail. From the red paper, cut 1 inner nose and 4 (1¾" x 9") strips. From the brown paper, cut 2 inner antlers, 1 inner head, 1 inner tail, and 4 (1½" x 9") strips. Cut 2 eyes from the yellow paper. Cut 2 pupils and 1 nose from the green paper. Cut 4 hooves from the black paper.

4. Center and glue 1 brown inner antler to 1 red antler. Repeat with the other red and brown antler. Center and glue the brown inner head to the red head and the brown inner tail to the red tail. Center and glue the pupils to the eyes and the red inner nose to the green nose. For the legs, center and glue 1 brown strip to 1 red strip. Glue the other leg strips in the same way.

5. To add the hooves, glue 1 hoof to 1 end of 1 leg strip. Let it dry. Fold the strip at 1″ intervals, accordion-style. Glue the brown side of the other end to the bottom of the box, using the photo as a guide. Repeat for the other legs.

6. Glue the brown side of the tail end to the bottom of the box.

7. To make the face, glue the nose, eyes, and antlers in place, using the photo as a guide. Glue the face to the box top.

8. To make the bow tie, fold the tissue paper into a 5″ square. Gather the square in the middle and tie it with the ribbon. Curl the ribbon ends with scissors. Glue the bow tie to the box lid below the face.

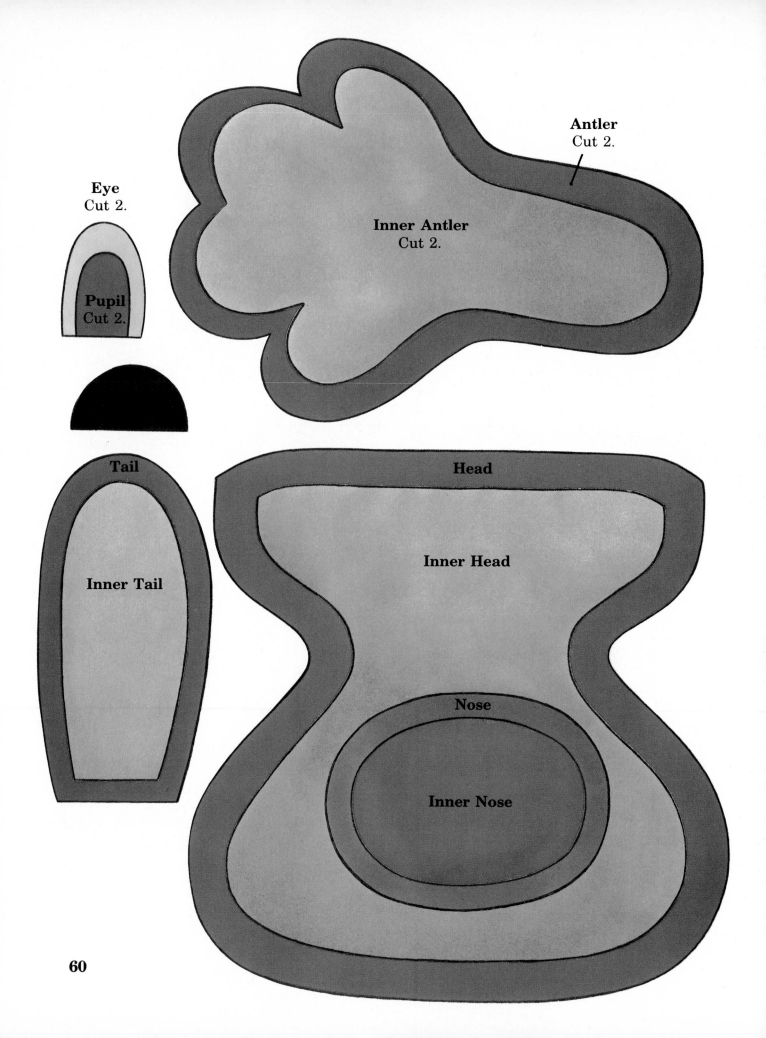

Eye
Cut 2.

Pupil
Cut 2.

Antler
Cut 2.

Inner Antler
Cut 2.

Tail

Inner Tail

Head

Inner Head

Nose

Inner Nose

60

Santa Sack

Make your holiday deliveries in style with this decorated sack. Or if you have a really big present, wrap it in tissue paper and drop it inside the sack. It makes a great wrap for surprises.

You will need:
Tracing paper and pencil
Scissors
Construction paper: red, yellow, green,
    black, white, brown, light pink, dark
    pink
2 large plain brown paper sacks
Glue
Ruler
Hole punch
Colored markers: black, brown, yellow,
    orange, pink
1 yard of heavy paper cording

1. Trace and cut out the patterns.

2. From red paper, cut out Santa's suit
and hat. From yellow paper, cut out the
moon, 1 large star, 1 medium star, and 4
small stars. From green paper, cut out
the tree and Santa's toy sack. From black
paper, cut out the 2 boots and the mitten.
From white paper, cut out Santa's beard
and hair, the pom-pom, and the dolls.
From brown paper, cut out the tree trunk.
From light pink paper, cut out Santa's
face. From dark pink, cut 1 cheek.

3. For the snowflakes, tear 17 small
pieces from the white paper.

4. Fold the upper edge of 1 sack down 2″
to the inside and glue it in place.

5. On the front of the sack, measure in
3½″ from each side and 1″ down from the
upper folded edge and mark. Use the hole
punch to make a hole at each mark. Repeat for the back of the sack.

6. To make the gift tag, place the brown
star pattern on a fold of the second grocery sack and trace around it. Cut the

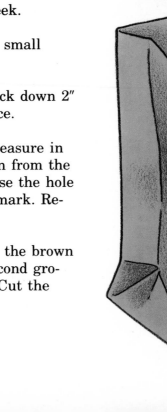

star out, being careful not to cut along the fold line. Glue the large yellow star to the front of the folded brown paper star. Use the hole punch to punch through all layers below the folded point.

7. Place Santa's suit on 1 side of the sack, as shown in the photograph. Place the boots under the lower edges of the legs. Place the mitten under the sleeve edge. Place the tree trunk under the mitten. Place the toy sack under the back of the suit. Glue each piece in place. Glue the face in place. Glue the pom-pom under the tip of the hat. Glue the hat in place. Place the tree on top of the trunk. Place a small star at the top of the tree. Place the beard/hair over the edges of the face and over the lower branch of the tree. Glue each piece in place. Glue the cheek above the beard.

8. Glue the snowflakes all over the front of the bag.

9. With the black marker, outline Santa's coat, sleeve, pants, and hat. With the brown marker, color the hair of 1 doll. With the yellow marker, color the hair of the other doll and the sleeves of the first doll. Color the sleeves of the second doll orange. With the pink marker, make circles for cheeks. Glue the dolls at the top of the toy sack.

10. Glue the moon and the medium star at the top of the bag. Glue 3 small stars to the bottom of Santa's suit.

11. To make the handles, cut the cording in half. Thread the gift tag onto 1 piece of the cording. Thread the ends of the cording through the holes on the front of the bag. Knot the ends on the inside of the bag. Repeat for the back handle.

Dolls

Hat

Santa's Face

Cheek

Beard/Hair

Pom-pom

Toy Sack

Santa's Suit

Mitten

Boot

Boot

64

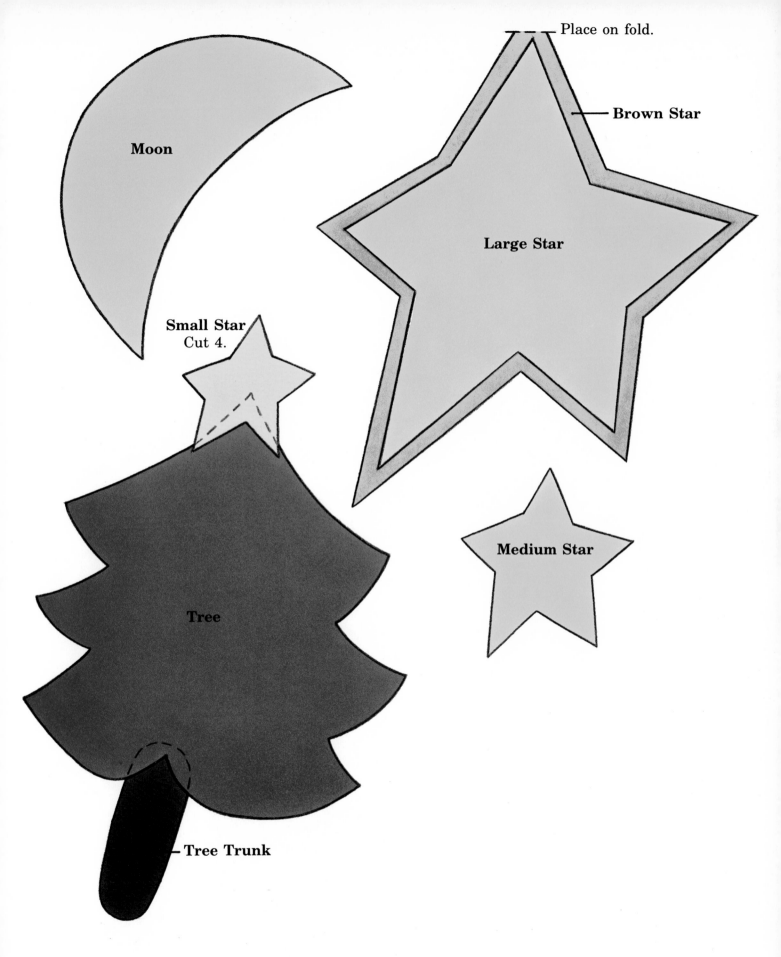

Moon

Place on fold.

Brown Star

Large Star

Small Star
Cut 4.

Medium Star

Tree

Tree Trunk

Pop-up Package Toppers

Snip, punch, and glue. These Christmas trees are easy to do. Cut them from white or colored pocket folders to make them really sturdy.

You will need (for 1 topper):
Tracing paper
Pencil
Scissors
Pocket folder
Tape
Hole punch
Glue

1. Trace and cut out the pattern. Be sure to mark the fold line.

2. Open up the pocket folder. Place the tree pattern on 1 pocket, lining up the fold line of the tree pattern with the bottom folded edge of the pocket. Trace around the pattern. Repeat with the other pocket.

3. Cut out the trees, being careful not to cut along the fold lines.

4. With the trees still folded, use the hole punch to punch out the ornament holes.

5. To make a 3-dimensional tree, glue 2 folded trees together along the folds. Let the glue dry.

6. Tape the package topper to your gift.

Tree
Cut 2 on fold.

Place on fold.

Copycat Cards

It's not often you want to be a copycat, but to make these cards that's just what you do. Trace a favorite photo of yourself. Then add some Christmas details like wreaths or ribbons to the picture. Make as many photocopies as you will need to send. Color each one and mail or deliver your handiwork.

You will need:
A grown-up
Photograph
Masking tape
Clear acetate
Fine-point black permanent marker
Cotton swabs and polish remover
Heavyweight paper: white, colored
Photocopy machine
Colored markers
Scissors
Glue
Envelopes to fit cards

1. Choose a photograph that shows faces close up.

2. Tape the edges of the photo to a flat surface. Lay the acetate over the photo and tape it down. Outline the faces and large shapes in the photograph with the permanent marker. If you make a mistake, dip a cotton swab in polish remover and rub until the marks are erased. Let the polish remover dry before you try again.

3. Add Christmas details with the marker. Let the ink dry before you untape the edges.

4. Ask the grown-up to help you put your white paper in the copier. Make as many copies as you need. To photocopy the drawing, lay the acetate face down on the copier glass and lay a sheet of white paper on top of it. If you want the drawing to be larger or smaller, check to see if the copier will do that. Make sure your drawing will fit in your envelope when trimmed and mounted on colored paper.

5. Color each drawing with the colored markers.

6. To finish the cards, decide if you want to make note cards or fold-over cards. For a note card, trim each photocopied drawing to the size you want. Glue the drawing to the colored paper. Trim the colored paper so that there is a ½″ border around the drawing. For a fold-over card, trim each drawing. Fold the colored paper in half widthwise and center the drawing on 1 side. Trim the colored paper, so that you have a ½″ border around the drawing. Glue the drawing to the colored paper.

7. Write your greeting on the back of the note card or inside the card.

Shadow Box Greetings

Christmas cheer comes in all shapes and sizes. This year, instead of a card, create a holiday scene in the bottom of a gift box. Then put on the lid and label, and your greetings are ready for delivery.

Snowman Box

You will need:
Poster paints: dark blue, white, red, green
Paintbrush
Small white gift box with lid
Fine-point permanent red marker
2 large white 2-hole buttons
Glue
Scrap of Christmas ribbon
9 tiny colored pom-poms
Piece of imitation greenery for tree
Rhinestone star
Cotton

1. Paint the bottom of the inside of the box blue and let it dry. Paint white snowflakes on the blue background. Let them dry. Paint the sides of the box on the inside and outside as shown. Let them dry.

2. Using the red marker, draw the snowman's hat and mouth on 1 button. (The eyes will be the holes.) Glue the buttons for the head and body to the blue bottom of the box. Let them dry.

3. Tie the ribbon in a knot and glue it to the snowman for a scarf. Glue 1 pom-pom to the top of the snowman's hat. Then glue on a pom-pom nose and pom-pom buttons. Let them dry.

4. Glue the greenery for the tree beside the snowman. Glue the star at the top of the tree. Glue on the pom-pom ornaments. Let them dry.

5. Glue the cotton across the base of the scene. Let it dry.

Manger Box

You will need:
Poster paints: light blue, yellow, red,
  blue, and green
Paintbrush
Small white gift box with lid
Fabric scrap
Glue
Small wooden doll pin (cut to 1¾″)
1 purple button for halo
Fine-point black marker
Packing straw
Rhinestone circles and star

1. Paint the bottom of the inside of the box light blue and let it dry. Paint the sides of the box as shown. Let them dry.

2. To make Baby Jesus, wrap the fabric scrap around the doll and glue the edges. Glue the button to the top of the doll's head for a halo. Let it dry.

3. Draw the eyes with the black marker.

4. Glue the straw across the base of the scene. Glue the doll on top of the straw. Let them dry.

5. Glue on the rhinestones. Let them dry.

Reindeer Box

You will need:
Poster paints: green, red
Paintbrush
Small white gift box with lid
Large brown 2-hole button for head
Glue
Tiny red pom-pom for nose
Small jingle bell
Scrap of Christmas ribbon
Small wooden spool
Brown watercolor paint
Twigs for antlers, tail, and legs
Rhinestone star
Small amount of Spanish moss

1. Paint the bottom of the inside of the box green and let it dry. Paint the sides of the box as shown. Let them dry.

2. Glue the button near the center of the box for the reindeer's head. (The eyes will be the holes.) Glue the pom-pom on for the nose. Let them dry.

3. Thread the bell onto the ribbon. Tie the ribbon in a knot and glue it below the button. Let it dry.

4. Lightly paint the spool with the brown watercolor. Let it dry. Glue the spool in place for the body and let it dry. Glue a tiny twig on for a tail.

5. Glue a twig on each side of the button for the antlers. Glue a twig on each end of the spool for the legs. Let them dry.

6. Glue the star in place. Let it dry.

7. Glue the moss across the base of the scene. Let it dry.

73

Kitty Cottage

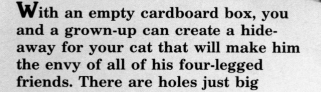

With an empty cardboard box, you and a grown-up can create a hide-away for your cat that will make him the envy of all of his four-legged friends. There are holes just big enough for paw games, a front door, and an escape hatch in the roof. There are even a few mice lurking about just for fun.

You will need:
A grown-up
Tracing paper
Pencil
Newspaper
17″ x 14½″ x 16″ cardboard box
Founder's Adhesive glue
Ruler
Scissors
Craft knife
Stencil letters (2″-high)
Acrylic paints: black, green, red
Paintbrushes

1. Trace the patterns and cut them out. Follow the instructions on the mouse body pattern to make the door pattern and the rooftop circle pattern.

2. If your box does not have printing on it, skip this step.

Ask the grown-up to help you carefully take the box apart by pulling up the glued flaps. Keep working until you have a flat box. Lay it down with the printed side facing up. Now, re-fold the flaps of

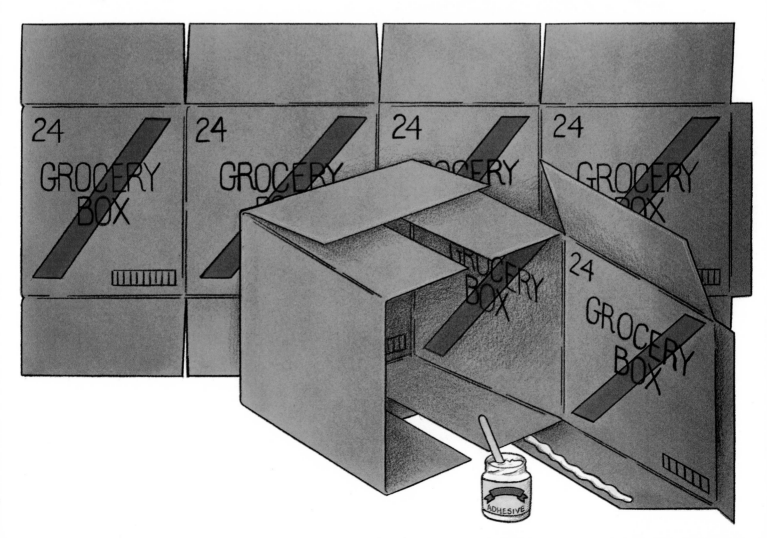

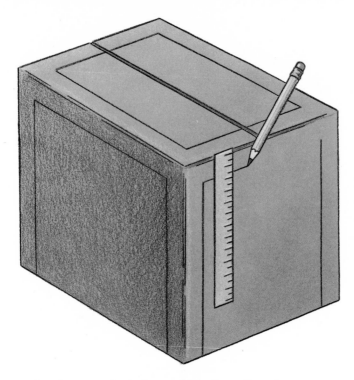

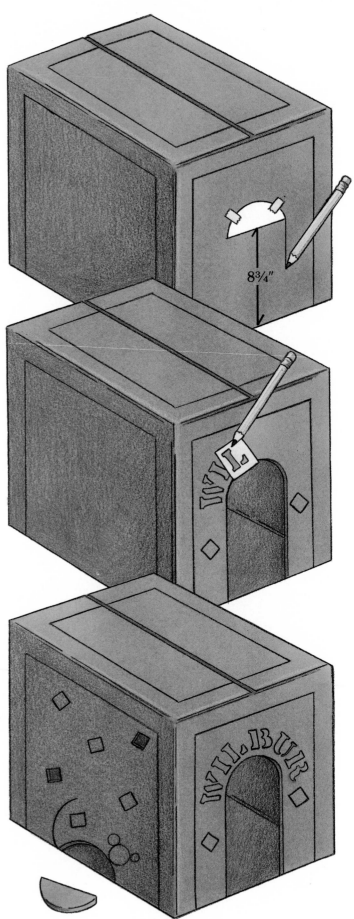

the box so that the printed surface is on the inside. Glue the bottom flaps together. Place 1 or 2 books on the glued flaps and let them dry. Repeat for the other flaps.

3. For the border around the top of the box, measure and draw a line 1½″ from the edge. Also draw lines 1½″ from all the other edges except the bottom.

4. Choose 1 end of the box to be the front. Line up the bottom of the door pattern 8¾″ above the bottom edge of the box. Tape the pattern in place and trace around the top. Continue your lines down each side as shown. **Ask the grown-up** to cut out the door. Trace around the square pattern 1 time on each side of the door. To stencil your cat's name, trace the stencil letters you need over the door.

5. To decorate the sides of the box, center the mouse pattern along the bottom edge of 1 side and trace around it. Trace around the square pattern to make 6 squares all around this side. **Ask the grown-up** to cut just the mouse body and 2 of the squares out of the box. Repeat for the opposite side of the box.

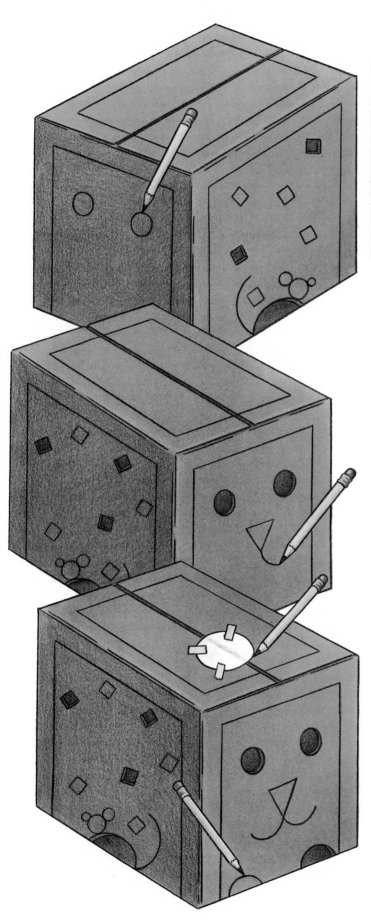

6. To decorate the back of the box, trace around the pattern for the cat's eye 2 times. **Ask the grown-up** to cut both eyes out of the box.

Center the top of the nose-mouth pattern below the eyes and trace around it. Place the paw pattern along the bottom edge and trace around it. Do the same thing for the other paw. **Ask the grown-up** to cut out the paws. Now trace 3 squares on the back of the box.

7. To decorate the top of the box, place the rooftop circle pattern near the back of the box and trace around it. Trace 4 squares on the top. **Ask the grown-up** to cut the circle and 1 square out of the box.

8. Cover your work area with newspaper. Use black paint to paint the letters over the door. Be careful not to use too much paint. Also paint the heads, noses, ears, and tails of the mice and the cat's nose and mouth black. Let the paint dry.

Paint all of the remaining squares green. Then paint the borders on the top and sides of the box red. Let the paint dry.

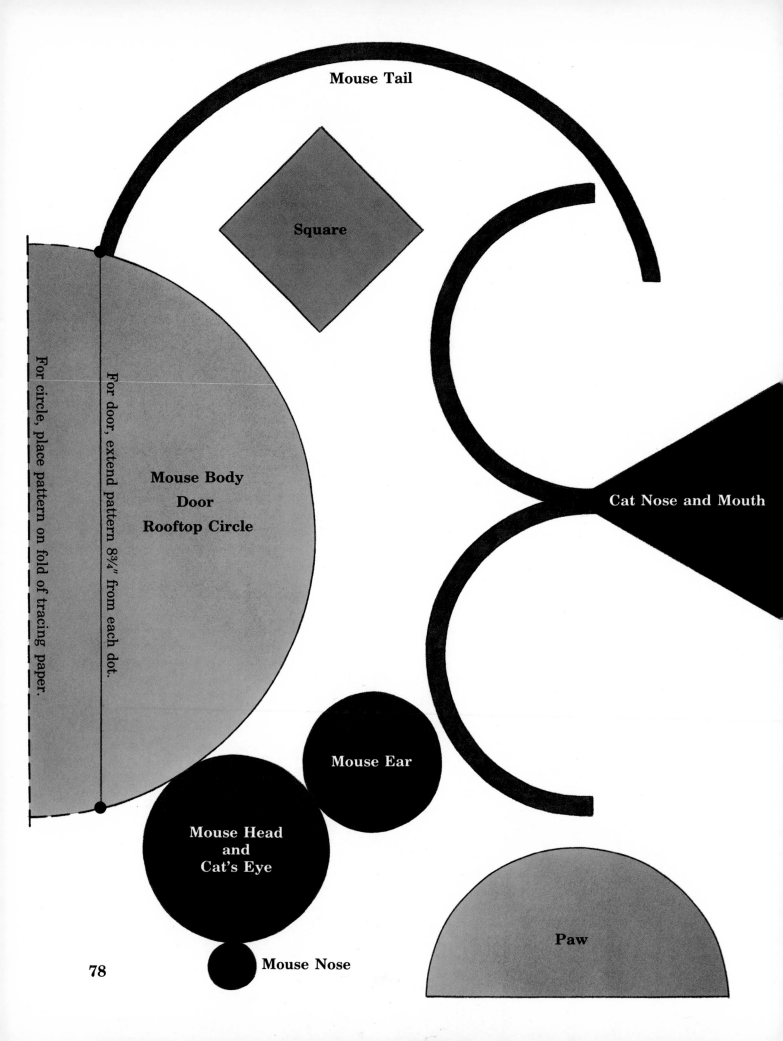

Mouse Tail

Square

For circle, place pattern on fold of tracing paper.

For door, extend pattern 8¾" from each dot.

Mouse Body
Door
Rooftop Circle

Cat Nose and Mouth

Mouse Ear

Mouse Head
and
Cat's Eye

Paw

78

Mouse Nose

Silly Pins

Make awesome pins for awesome friends! Gather together miniature toys and trinkets and glue them inside acrylic boxes. Each pin will be as unique as its maker.

You will need (for each pin):
Small acrylic craft box
Founder's Adhesive glue
Pin back

For sunglasses pin:
7″ strips of crinkle ribbon
Small sunglasses pins

For clown pin:
Flat-tailed plastic fishing worms
Plastic bead necklace
Scissors
Shoelace curl
Miniature clown head

For jewel pin:
Colored shredded paper
3 costume-jewel rings

Sunglasses Pin

1. Coat the inside of the box with glue. Press 1 end of each piece of crinkle ribbon into the box so that the ribbon sticks to the glue. Let the ribbon ends dangle over the edge of the box.

2. Pin the sunglasses pins to the crinkle ribbons.

3. Glue the pin back to the back of the box. Let it dry.

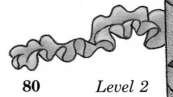

Clown Pin

1. Coat the inside of the box with glue.

2. Press the heads of the worms into the box so that they stick to the glue. Let the tails dangle over the edge of the box.

3. Cut the necklace into 3 or 4 pieces. (If the necklace isn't knotted between beads you'll need to knot the ends of the cut pieces.) Glue each piece in the box so that the ends dangle over the edge.

4. Glue the clown head to the shoelace curl. Glue the curl in the center of the box.

5. Glue the pin back to the back of the box. Let it dry.

Jewel Pin

1. Coat the inside of the box with glue.

2. Press the shredded paper into the box so that it sticks to the glue and the ends dangle over the edges.

3. Glue the rings in the center of the paper.

4. Glue the pin back to the back of the box. Let it dry.

Cigar Boxes

Everybody needs a place to store small treasures, and cigar boxes are perfect for the job. Ask for them at a local specialty shop or drug store. Then select wrapping paper to decorate each box.

You will need (for 1 box):
Tracing paper
Pencil
Ruler
Tape measure
Cigar box
Wrapping paper
Scissors
Glue stick
4″ piece of ribbon
Founder's Adhesive glue

1. To cover the cigar box, trace inside the borders of the top and the sides of the box on tracing paper. Cut out these shapes and use them as patterns. Trace around each pattern on the wrong side of the wrapping paper. Cut the pieces out.

2. If the sides of the box do not have borders or if you want to cover the borders, use the tape measure to measure around all 4 sides of the box. Then measure the height of 1 side. Use these measurements to draw your shape directly onto the wrong side of the wrapping paper. Cut it out.

3. Glue each piece in place with the glue stick.

4. Measure the inside of the box lid and draw that shape on the wrong side of the wrapping paper. Cut it out and glue it in place.

5. For the pull tab, fold the ribbon in half with the short ends together. Glue them together with Founder's Adhesive.

6. Glue the ends of the tab on the center of the inside top of the box using Founder's Adhesive. Let it dry.

Cinnamon Baskets

Five, six, pick up sticks—cinnamon sticks, that is. Glue them around a can, and you'll have a sweet-smelling basket ready to be filled with holiday treats.

You will need (for 1 basket):
A grown-up
3½" x 2" food can
Founder's Adhesive glue
35 (4") cinnamon sticks
1 yard (1"-wide) grosgrain ribbon
Individually wrapped candies

1. **Ask the grown-up** to remove the top and the label from the can. Be careful handling any rough edges. Wash the can and let it dry.

2. Apply the glue to the outside of the can, covering the sides completely.

3. Place 1 cinnamon stick on the side of the can, making sure the bottom of the stick is even with the bottom edge of the can. Continue gluing the sticks in place, 1 at a time, until the sides are covered.

4. To decorate, tie the ribbon around the sticks and into a bow. Trim the ribbon ends at an angle. Fill the basket with candy.

Level 2

Nativity Shadow Puppets

Gather one and all for a very special production of the Christmas story. Light up your handmade stage and shadow puppets by placing a desk lamp behind the stage. Your own narration will make this presentation a holiday treat.

You will need:
Tracing paper and pencil
Scissors
2 sheets of blue posterboard
12″ of florist's wire
Glue
8 popsicle sticks
Black sewing thread
Yardstick

Clear tape
Glue stick
Colored tissue paper: 2 sheets of purple, 1
    sheet of pink
9 Velcro dots with adhesive backs
Scrap of gold wrapping paper
Gold star stickers
2 (22″) pieces of ¾″ screen molding

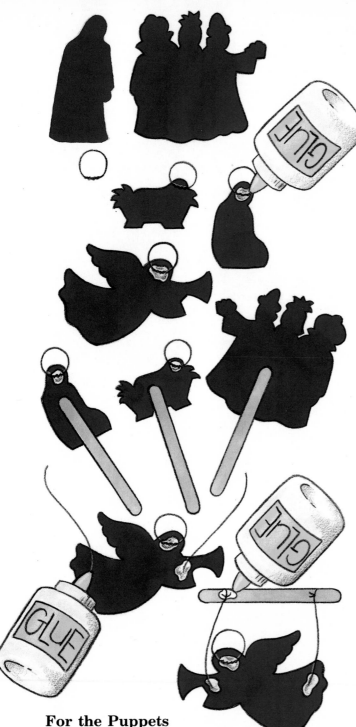

3. Glue the ends of the popsicle sticks to the backs of all the puppets except the angels. Cut 4 (6″) pieces of thread. On the back of 1 angel, glue the end of 1 thread behind the arms. Glue another behind the skirt. Tie the other ends of the threads to a popsicle stick. Put a dab of glue over the knots to hold them in place. Attach the thread to the other angel the same way but reverse the angel so that they face each other when you hang them.

For the Stage

1. See pages 92 and 93 for the patterns for the stage. Trace the patterns onto tracing paper and cut them out.

2. To make the stage, make a mark 8½″ from 1 end of the second sheet of poster-board. Use the yardstick to draw a line all the way across the posterboard. Also measure and draw a line 8½″ from the opposite end. Crease the posterboard along these lines.

3. For the left panel, line up the left edge of the panel pattern with the left edge of the posterboard and the top of the pattern 2½″ below the top edge of the pos-terboard. Tape the pattern in place on the posterboard. Trace around the palm tree and the white area. Cut out the white area. For the right panel, flip the pattern over and line it up with the right side of the posterboard just as you did for the left. Cut out the white area.

4. For the center section of the stage, line up the left edge of the center pattern with the left crease in the posterboard and the top of the pattern 1½″ below the top of the posterboard. Tape the pattern

For the Puppets

1. See pages 93 and 94 for the patterns for the puppets. Trace the patterns onto 1 sheet of posterboard and cut them out.

2. From the wire, cut a 3″ piece. Bend it in a circle to make a halo. Glue it to the back of Baby Jesus' head. Make 3 more halos. Glue them to the backs of the heads of Mary and the angels.

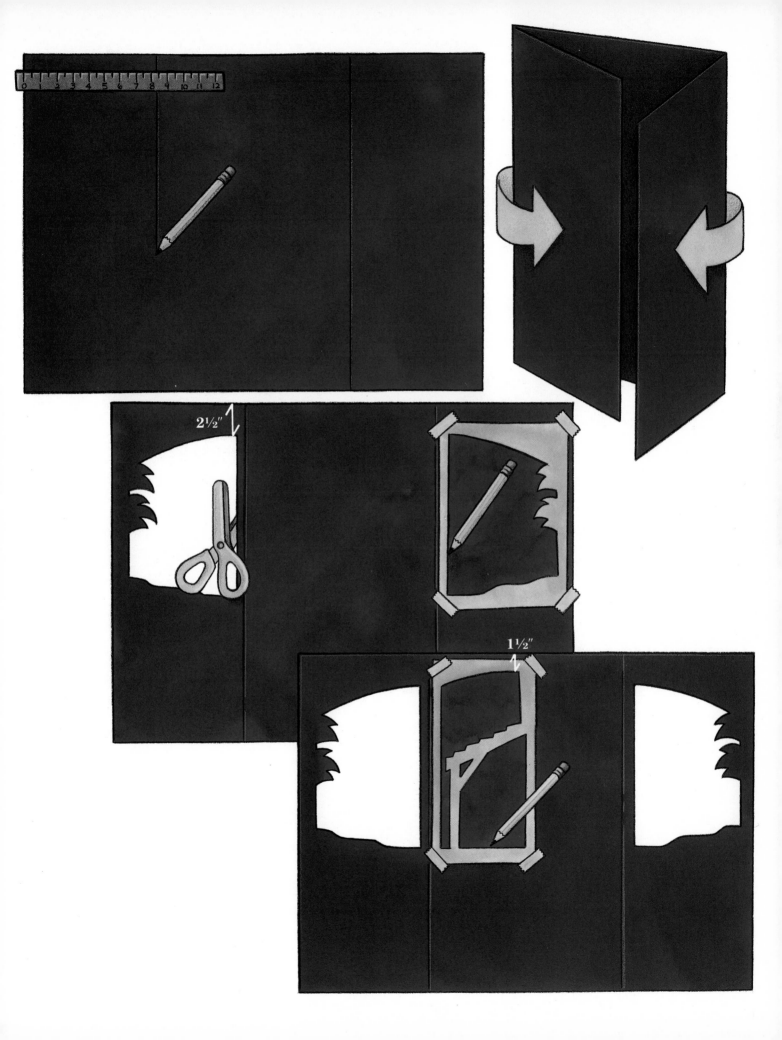

2½"

1½"

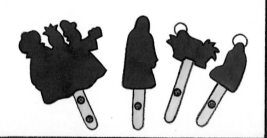

in place. Trace around the pattern. Then flip the pattern over. Line up the center lines and trace the other half. Cut out the white areas.

5. Rub the glue stick along the edge of the opening on the back of the left panel. Stretch a piece of purple tissue paper over the opening and press it down. Cut away the extra tissue around the edges. Glue the purple tissue paper to the back of the right panel in the same way.

Rub the glue stick along the sides of the stable. Stretch the pink tissue paper over this area and press it down. Trim the excess paper so that it doesn't stick out from behind the stable. Cover the remaining open area with purple tissue paper. Trim the edges where necessary.

6. Use the Velcro dots to hold the puppets in place while the play is in progress. Place the sticky side of 1 dot on the front of each puppet's popsicle stick. Place 2 dots on the Wise Men for extra support. Decide where you want the figures to stand and stick the corresponding dots to the back of the stage.

7. Trace the star pattern on the gold paper and cut it out. On the front of the stage, center and glue the star over the stable. Stick the small star stickers on the tissue paper in the side panels.

8. To help support the stage, glue 1 piece of molding to the back of the left panel on the stage. Glue the other piece of molding to the back of the right panel.

Left Panel Pattern

Place 2½″ from the top of the posterboard.
Turn over for the right panel pattern.

Cut out white area.

Star

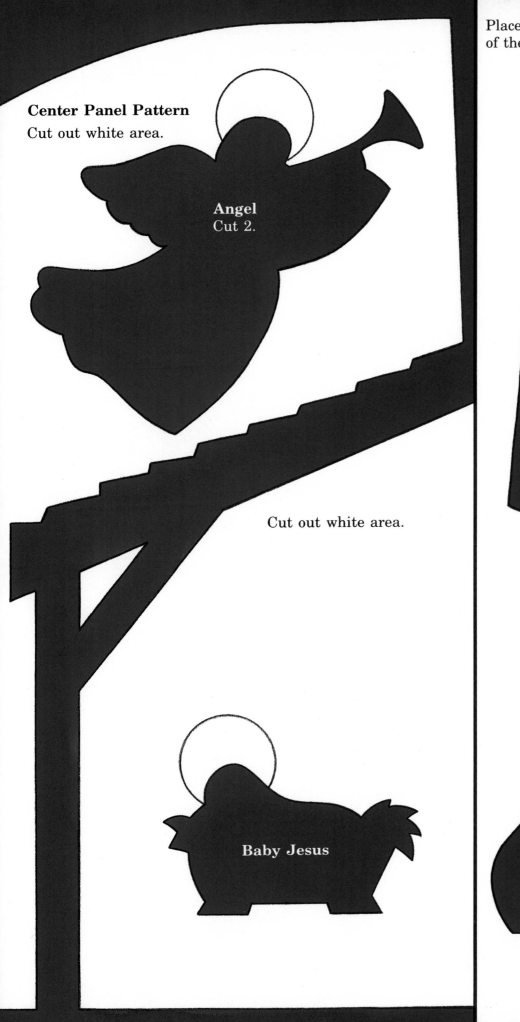

Center Panel Pattern
Cut out white area.

Angel
Cut 2.

Cut out white area.

Baby Jesus

Place 1½″ below the top of the posterboard.

Joseph

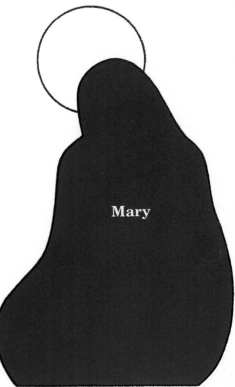

Mary

Lamb

Donkey

Shepherd

Three Wise Men

Lace Doily Frames

You've probably used paper doilies to make Valentines. This Christmas use a doily to frame a favorite photo. Take a trip to the dime store or kitchen shop to discover all the assorted sizes and shapes of doilies available.

You will need:
Colored posterboard
Pencil
Ruler
Assorted sizes of paper doilies
Scissors
Photograph
Glue
Cellophane tape

Square Frame

1. On the posterboard, trace around the square doily 2 times. Cut out the squares.

2. Measure the area of the photograph you want to frame. Then draw a square that size in the center of the doily and cut it out.

3. Place the doily on 1 posterboard square, lining up all the edges. Trace the opening in the doily onto the posterboard and cut it out. Use this piece of posterboard for the front of the frame.

4. Line up the edges of the doily and the front of the frame. Glue them together and let them dry.

5. Place the photo behind the opening. When it's in the right place, tape the edges of the photo to the back of the posterboard. Glue the other posterboard square to the back of the frame front.

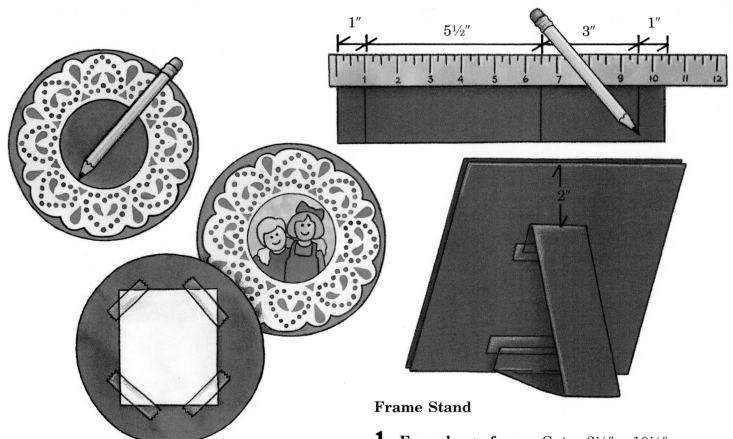

Round Frame

1. On the posterboard, trace around the round doily 2 times. Cut out the circles.

2. Measure the area of the photograph you want to frame. Then draw a circle that size in the center of the doily and cut it out.

3. Place the doily on 1 posterboard circle, lining up all the edges. Trace the opening in the doily onto the posterboard and cut it out. Use this piece of posterboard for the front of the frame.

4. Line up the edges of the doily and the front of the frame. Glue them together and let them dry.

5. Place the photo behind the opening. When it's in the right place, tape the edges of the photo to the back of the posterboard. Glue the other posterboard circle to the back of the frame front.

Frame Stand

1. For a large frame: Cut a 2½" x 10½" strip of posterboard. Measure 1" from 1 end. Draw a line across the posterboard. Measure 5½" from this line and draw another line. Measure 3" and draw another line.

2. Fold and crease the posterboard strip along each line. Turn under and tape 1 end to the back of the frame about 2" from the top. Turn under and line up the other end with the bottom of the frame. Tape the end to the frame as shown.

3. For a small frame: Cut a 1¼" x 6½" strip of posterboard. Measure 1" from 1 end. Draw a line across the posterboard. Measure 3" from this line and draw another line. Measure 1½" and draw another line.

4. Fold and crease the posterboard strip along each line. Tape 1 end to the back of the frame about 1" from the top. Line up the other end with the bottom of the frame. Tape the end to the frame.

Button Covers

Is there a fashion-minded female on your Christmas list? Why not create a set of unique button covers just for her. She can slip them on over the buttons on a shirt or sweater for the latest look.

You will need (for a set of 5):
5 button covers
5 decorative objects with flat backs:
   shells, or plastic stars, fish, and birds
Acrylic paint
Paintbrush
Silicone glue

1. Find some cute objects, with flat backs, that you'd like to turn into button covers! Check the shirt or sweater on which you think your friend will wear the button covers. Count the number of buttons to figure the number of button covers needed.

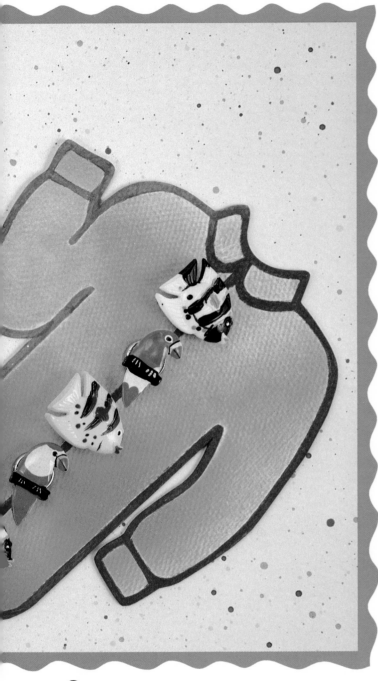

2. If you want, paint details or paint the entire object.

3. Glue 1 object to the top of 1 button cover. Let dry. Repeat with the remaining objects.

Fruit Place Mats

To design place mats for your mom this Christmas, you don't have to look far for inspiration. Take a peek at the fruit or vegetables in the refrigerator. Then look at Mom's dishes or the colors in your kitchen to help you decide what paint colors to use.

You will need (for 4 mats):
¾ yard (45"-wide) primed canvas or purchased pre-cut oval canvas mats
Glue
Acrylic paints: light green, green, purple, turquoise, red, yellow, black, white (or colors of your choice)
Paintbrushes
Clear acrylic spray coating

1. To make the rectangular mats, cut 4 (13″ x 18″) rectangles from the canvas. Turn under ½″ along 1 edge of 1 rectangle and glue it to the back. Place a heavy book on the edge to help make it stick. Let it dry. Glue under the remaining 3 edges. Glue the edges of the other rectangles the same way. Let them dry.

2. With a pencil, lightly draw your fruit or vegetable in the center of each place mat. Draw border designs around the outside edge of the mats.

3. Begin painting the bigger shapes. Let 1 color dry before painting another color on top of it. Wash your brush before changing colors and dry it with a paper towel. If you make a mistake, paint over it with the white paint. Let the white paint dry and then repaint with the first color. Let the place mats dry completely.

4. Apply 1 coat of acrylic spray to each mat and let it dry. Spray again and let the mats dry.

Parents' Workshop
Great Gifts for Children

Snowman Sweatshirt

You don't have to wait for the first snowfall to build this snowman. Just stencil the hat and the smile on a white sweatshirt and fill in with buttons and ribbons. Add white sweatpants, and you'll have the cutest snowman or snowgirl this season.

You will need:

Tracing paper
Clear acetate
Permanent marker
Cutting board
Craft knife
Hole punch
Cardboard square (large enough to stretch
   shirt slightly)
Masking tape
White sweatshirt and pants
Black fabric paint
Paper plate
Sponge
Grosgrain ribbon: 3″ (1½″-wide) orange,
   4″ (⅞″-wide) black-and-red confetti dot,
   9″ (1½″-wide) black-and-red polka-dot,
   2″ (⅜″-wide) black-and-red swiss dot
Straight pin
Liquid ravel preventer
Fabric glue
2 (1⅛″) square black buttons
Thread: orange, red, black
Safety pin

1. Trace the entire design onto tracing paper.

2. Place the traced design under a sheet of acetate and trace the hat and smile with the permanent marker.

3. To make the stencil, place the acetate on the cutting board. Cut out the hat with the craft knife. Use the hole punch to punch out the smile.

4. To smooth the shirt front for painting, place the cardboard inside the shirt. Tape the stencil to the front of the shirt.

5. Pour some of the fabric paint onto the paper plate. Using the sponge, apply the black paint to the cutout areas. (Paint the entire hat black. The hatband ribbon will be added later.) Before removing the stencil, let the paint dry according to the manufacturer's directions. If the design is not dark enough, apply a second coat of paint. Remove the stencil when the paint is completely dry.

6. To make the carrot nose, fold the orange ribbon in half lengthwise and pin. Use a ruler to draw a diagonal line from the outside corner to the opposite folded corner. Cut on the line through both thicknesses. Remove the pin and unfold.

7. Apply liquid ravel preventer to the cut edges of the orange ribbon (nose) and the confetti dot ribbon (hatband).

8. Apply fabric glue to the wrong side of the hatband and the wrong side of the nose. Referring to the photo, position them on the sweatshirt.

9. With matching thread, topstitch the hatband to the hat across the top and bottom of the hatband. Machine-appliqué around all 3 sides of the nose. Sew on the button eyes.

10. To make the bow tie, stitch the ends of the polka-dot ribbon together, forming a circle. Pinch the center of the ribbon circle together, forming 2 loops. Stitch through the pinched center to secure. Wrap the ⅜″ swiss dot ribbon around the center and stitch the ends to secure. Center the seam in back of the bow. Center the bow 2″ below the snowman's smile and safety-pin it in place.

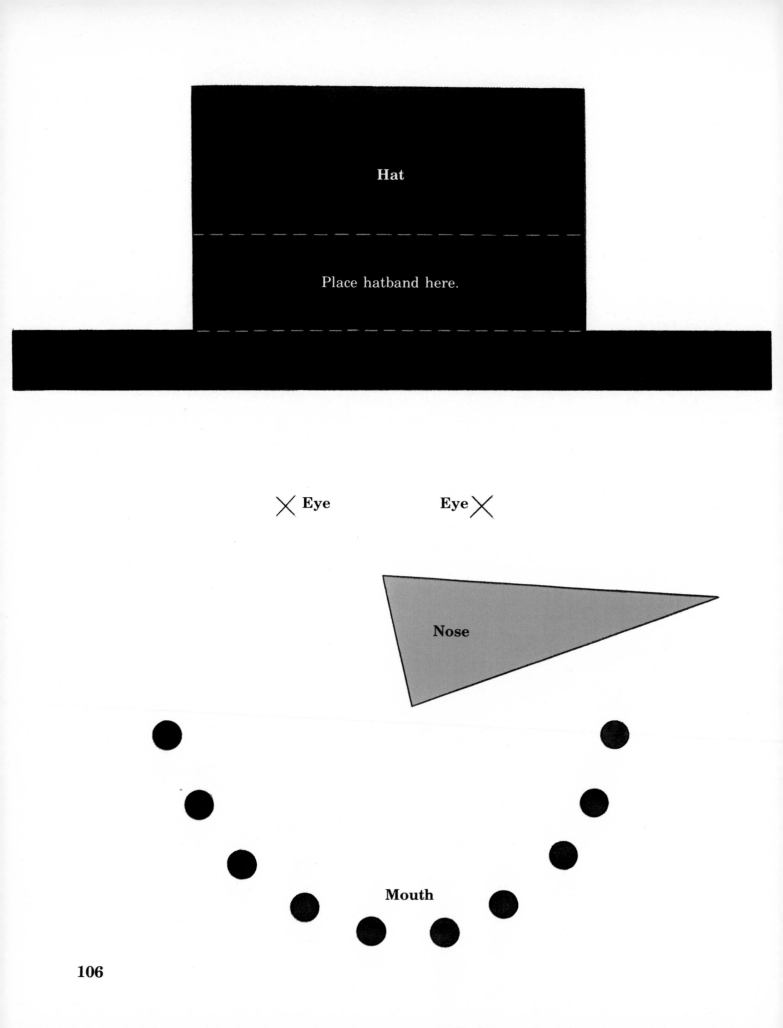

Hat

Place hatband here.

Eye   Eye

Nose

Mouth

Bathtime Trio

Splish, splash! When it's time for a bath, your favorite little girl will create waves in this colorful trio. Ribbon polka dots and stripes dress up this bathtime ensemble.

Bath Wrap

You will need:
Purchased white bath towel
Thread to match
⅔ yard (1″-wide) elastic
4½″ of Velcro tape
Grosgrain ribbon: ⅔ yard (1½″-wide)
  pink-and-white stripe, ¼ yard
  (1½″-wide) green swiss dot, ⅞ yard
  (1½″-wide) pink swiss dot

1. To make a casing for the elastic, fold under 1¼″ on 1 long edge of the towel. (This will be the top of the wrap.) Measure 5″ from 1 end and mark with a pin. Place a pin 5″ from the opposite end. Topstitch the bottom edge of the casing between the pins.

Cut a piece of elastic about 5″ shorter than the girl's chest measurement. Fasten a safety pin at 1 end of the elastic and run the elastic through the casing. Stitch 1 end of the elastic at each end of the casing.

2. To make the fastener for the wrap, stitch 1 piece of the Velcro to the inside of the towel on the right-hand side, lining up 1 end of the Velcro with the right-hand edge of the wrap and the other end with the end of the casing. Sew the other piece of the Velcro to the outside of the towel, lining up 1 end with the left-hand edge of the wrap.

3. For the front, place pins on the right-hand edge, 1½″ from the top and ½″ from the bottom. Cut a piece of striped ribbon the length between the pins plus 1″. Turn under ½″ on each end of the ribbon.

Placing 1 end of the ribbon 1½″ below the top edge of the wrap, align 1 edge of the ribbon ¾″ from the right-hand edge of the front of the wrap. Topstitch the ribbon in place along both sides.

4. To make the leaf for the rosette, cut the green ribbon into 2 (4″) pieces. With right sides facing, stitch them together along 1 long edge and 1 end. Turn the ribbon right side out and form a point at the sewn end. Run a gathering thread along the cut end of the ribbon, gather, and tack the leaf to the top left edge of the striped ribbon.

5. To make the rosette, fold 1 end of the pink swiss dot ribbon under ¼″ and tack in place. Then run a gathering thread along 1 long edge of the ribbon and gather. Fold the other end under ¼″ and tack in place.

6. Twist the ribbon into a spiral circle with 3 layers, making each layer slightly smaller than the 1 below. Tack the layers in place.

7. Tack the rosette in the center of the striped ribbon, covering the raw end of the leaf.

Flip-flops

You will need:
Purchased flip-flops
Grosgrain ribbon: 2 yards (¼″-wide)
  pink-and-white stripe, ⅜ yard
  (1½″-wide) green swiss dot, 1¼ yards
  (1½″-wide) pink swiss dot
Hot-glue gun and glue sticks
Thread to match ribbons

1. Cut the striped ribbon in half. To cover the straps on 1 flip-flop, thread the end of 1 piece of ribbon from the top through 1 back opening where the straps are attached to the sole. Glue the end of the ribbon to the sole. Wrap the ribbon around the strap, around the front thong, and around the rest of the strap, until the

straps are completely covered. Then slip the remaining ribbon end through the opening in the sole on the other side and glue the end in place. Trim any excess ribbon. Repeat for the other flip-flop.

2. To make the leaves for 1 flip-flop, cut a 6½″ piece from the green ribbon. With right sides facing, fold the ribbon lengthwise. Stitch across both ends. Turn the ribbon right side out and form a point at each end. Make leaves for the other flip-flop in the same way.

3. For the rosettes, cut the pink swiss dot ribbon into 2 (22″) pieces. For each piece, follow the instructions in step 5 of the bath wrap.

Twist the ribbon into a spiral circle with 2 layers, making the top layer slightly smaller than the 1 below. Tack the layers in place. Repeat to make the second rosette.

4. Glue the leaves to the center of the straps above the thong. Glue the rosette to the leaves. Repeat this step for the second flip-flop.

Headband

You will need:
6″ x 30″ piece of white terry cloth
Thread to match
Grosgrain ribbon: ¼ yard (1½″-wide) green swiss dot, ⅞ yard (1½″-wide) pink-and-white stripe
⅔ yard (1″-wide) elastic

1. Stitch together the short ends of the terry cloth to form a circle. With right sides facing, fold the long edges together and stitch, leaving a 2″ opening. Turn right side out through the opening.

2. Cut a piece of elastic the circumference of the child's head minus 1″. Fasten a safety pin at 1 end of the elastic and run it through the terry cloth tube. Overlap the ends of the elastic and stitch them together. Let the elastic slip into the band. Slipstitch the opening closed.

3. To make the leaves, cut a 6½″ piece of green ribbon and follow the instructions in step 2 of the flip-flops. Gather the ribbon in the center.

4. To make the rosette, follow the instructions in steps 5 and 6 of the bath wrap.

5. Sew the center of the leaf to the center seam of the headband. Tack the rosette to the center of the leaves.

Wild 'n Wooly Headbands

Everybody on the party line is sure to agree—these headbands will be the last word in cold-weather head gear. Lined with fleece, they'll keep ears stylishly warm this winter.

You will need (for each):
Tape measure
Tracing paper
Water-soluble marker
Mediumweight fusible interfacing
⅛ yard of fleece
⅛ yard of print fabric
Contrasting thread
Thread to match beads
2″ square of Velcro

For the paw:
Scrap of red fabric
Thread to match

For the swan:
Scraps of orange and teal fabric
Thread to match
1 small black bead
3 small red beads
Purple embroidery floss

For the lion:
1 (1½″) pom-pom
2 small black beads

For the bunny:
1 (1½″) pom-pom
2 small black beads

1. Measure the circumference of the child's head. (The circumference of most heads will range from 20-22″.)

2. Trace the patterns for the headband and any appliqué pieces. Extend the headband pattern to the desired length (the circumference of the child's head plus 3″). Cut out the patterns. Transfer the pattern and all the details to the fabric

with the water-soluble marker. (Do not cut out yet.)

3. Following the manufacturer's instructions, fuse the interfacing to the wrong side of the fabric.

4. Pin the wreath and bill on the swan and machine-appliqué them in place. With the embroidery floss, satin-stitch the heart on the cheek. For the paw, pin the heart and machine-appliqué it in place.

5. Pin the fleece to the back of the headband, with wrong sides facing. With contrasting thread, zigzag the fabric and fleece together on all the lines marked on the fabric. Cut out the headband and fleece. To reduce bulk at the edge of the headband, trim the fleece at an angle.

6. Zigzag around the headband and along all the details again for complete coverage.

7. Zigzag the hook side of the Velcro square to the fabric side of the plain end of the headband. By hand, sew the loop side of the Velcro square to the fleece side of the decorative end of the headband. Be sure to stitch only through the fleece, not through the fabric.

8. Stitch the pom-poms on the bunny and lion for tails. With black thread, sew on the black beads for eyes. For the swan, sew on red beads for holly.

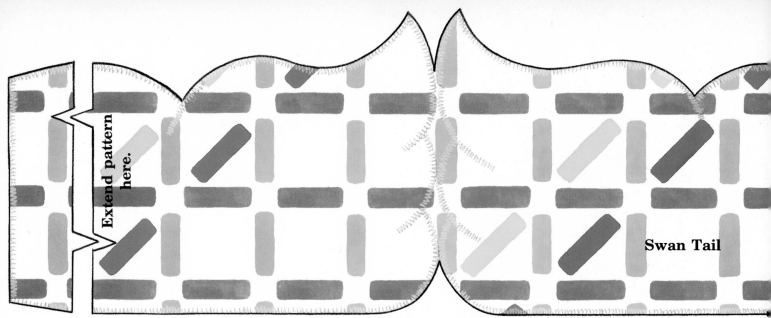

Extend pattern here.

Swan Tail

Place in the center
of headband.

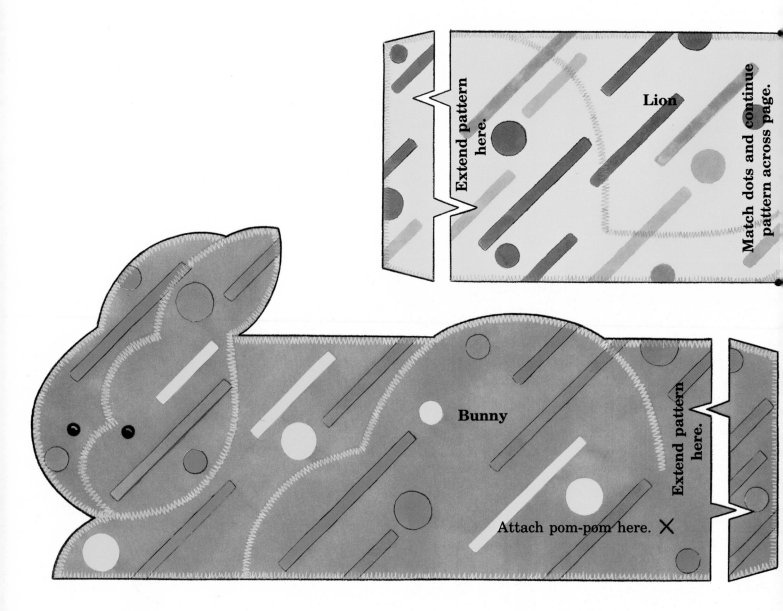

Extend pattern here.

Lion

Match dots and continue pattern across page.

Bunny

Extend pattern here.

Attach pom-pom here. ✕

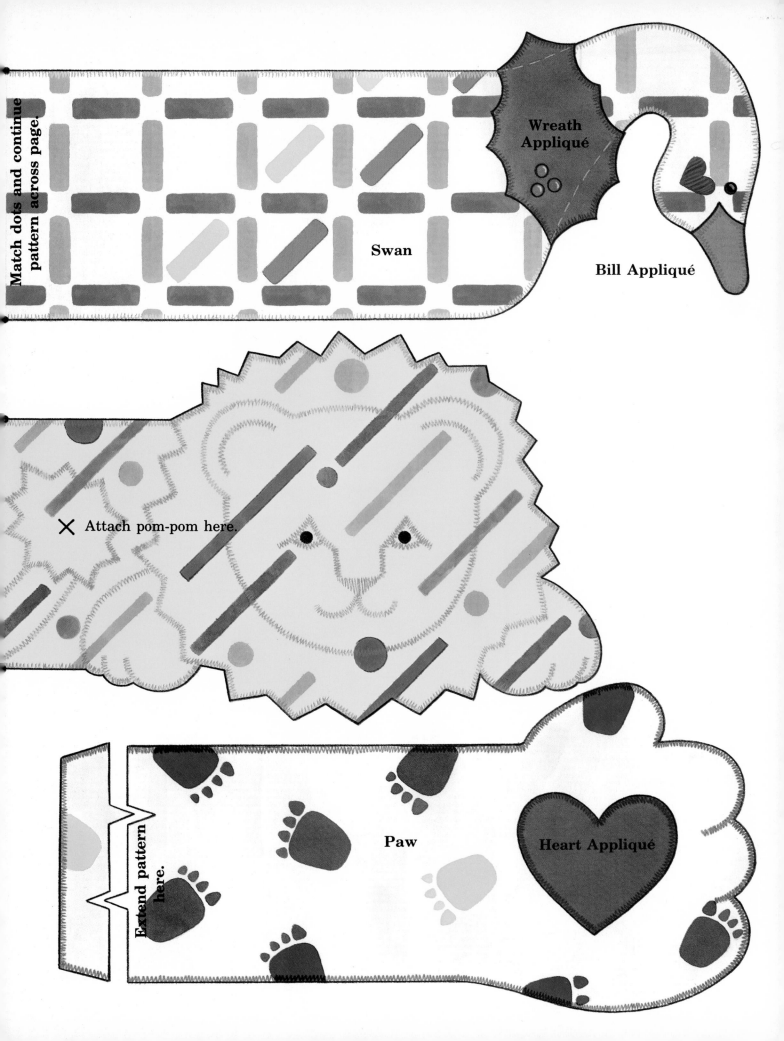

Match dots and continue pattern across page.

Wreath Appliqué

Swan

Bill Appliqué

✕ Attach pom-pom here.

Extend pattern here.

Paw

Heart Appliqué

Team Tees

Picture this— your child's team on a T-shirt! Select the best team photo and a plain white T-shirt. Then get to work on a project kids will enjoy showing off everywhere they go.

You will need (for 1 shirt):
T-shirt
Photograph
Photocopy machine
T-shirt board or piece of cardboard
Plastic wrap
Clear tape
Straight pins
Scissors
Wax paper
2 (1″) foam brushes
"Picture This" transfer medium for fabric
Paper towels
Rolling pen
Sponge
Fabric paint

1. Before you begin, wash and dry the T-shirt.

2. Make a color or black-and-white photocopy of your photograph. Though you may enlarge your photograph to any size, 8½″ x 11″ or smaller will be the easiest to work with.

3. To transfer the photocopy to the shirt, follow the manufacturer's instructions on "Picture This" transfer medium. (We have listed the supplies that the manufacturer's instructions call for.)

4. With a foam brush and fabric paint, add colored borders to each side of photo.

115

Argyle Sweater

This sweater is perfect for young golfers on or off the green. And it's right on course for even the busiest of moms because the design is duplicate-stitched on a purchased sweater. So, Mom, send them to the links in style.

You will need:

Purchased blue sweater with a gauge of
  6½ stitches and 11 rows = 1″
DMC matte cotton yarn (11-yard skeins):
  4 skeins yellow #2444, 2 skeins fuchsia
  #2326, 1 skein black #2310
Tapestry needle

1. At the center front of the sweater,
using the tapestry needle, begin stitching
the yellow diamond just below the neck-
band. Duplicate-stitch the design following the chart and color code, using 1
strand of DMC yarn. (See Figures A and
B.) Stitch all the solid diamonds first.
Then stitch the entire black outline.

2. Repeat the design down the center
front of the sweater to the waistband.

Duplicate Stitch

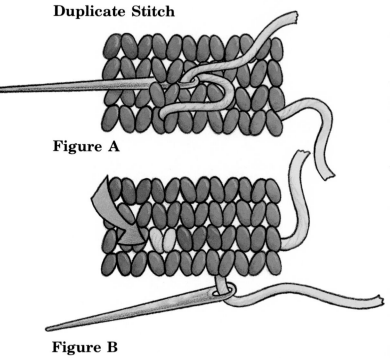

Figure A

Figure B

**Stitch Count (for duplicate-stitch
design): 41 x 142**

Party Purses

No time to sew? You can still whip up these pretty party purses. They're no-sew fashions just right for accessorizing a young lady's favorite party outfit.

You will need (for 1 purse):
1 (8½″ x 19″) piece of colored mylar tissue paper
⅔ yard (36″-wide) clear, mediumweight vinyl
Iron and pressing cloth
Hole punch
1 yard (⅛″) iridescent cording
1″ Velcro dot with adhesive back
1 flat decorative button
Glue

1. To make the pointed envelope flap for the purse, mark both long sides of the colored paper 6″ from 1 end. Mark the center of that end. Draw lines from the center mark to the marks on the sides. Cut the paper along these 2 lines.

2. Cut the vinyl into 2 (10″ x 20″) pieces. Center the colored paper between the 2 pieces of vinyl. Trim the vinyl, following the shape of the paper, but leave ¼″ margins of vinyl on all sides.

3. To seal the edges of the vinyl, use a pressing cloth and press 1 edge with a medium-hot iron. Press for about 15 seconds. Repeat until all the edges are melted together. Let cool.

4. To shape the purse, fold the straight end up 7″, aligning the sides. To seal each side, use a pressing cloth and press just the edges with a medium-hot iron for about 15 seconds until they are melted together. Let cool.

5. With the hole punch, punch a hole ½″ from 1 side and just below the opening of the purse. Repeat for the other side.

6. For the shoulder strap, cut the cording to the desired length. Thread the ends of the cording through the holes. Tie the ends in double knots.

7. Peel off the backs of the Velcro closure. Fold the pointed flap down, covering the purse opening. Apply 1 Velcro dot to the back of the flap and 1 to the front of the purse, aligning the 2 pieces.

8. Glue the button on the front of the flap.

Clothes Trees

When it's time for little cowboys to bed down and bunnies to burrow, they need a place to hang their hats and rest their ears. You'll find these clothes trees a great place to keep the ranch and farm in order until early morning.

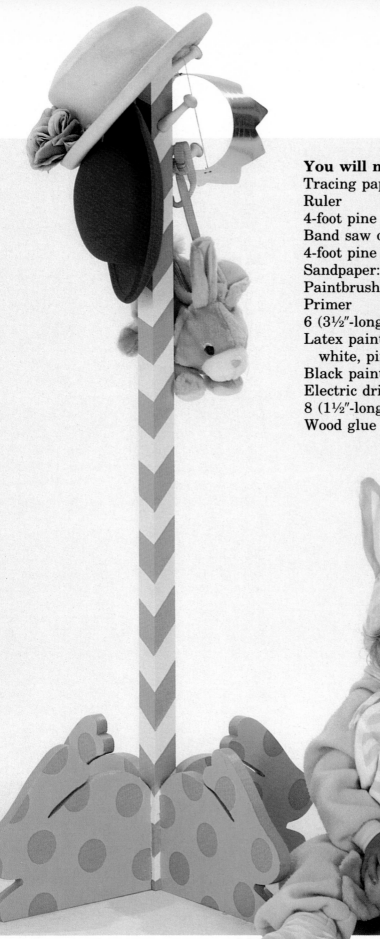

You will need (for 1 clothes tree):
Tracing paper
Ruler
4-foot pine 1 x 12
Band saw or jigsaw
4-foot pine 2 x 2
Sandpaper: medium, fine grade
Paintbrushes
Primer
6 (3½″-long) ½″ wooden pegs
Latex paints: white, black, red for cow;
    white, pink, green for bunny
Black paint pen for cow
Electric drill with ⅜″ and ½″ bits
8 (1½″-long) ⅜″ wooden dowels
Wood glue

1. Enlarge the desired pattern and cut it out.

2. Trace the pattern 4 times on the 1 x 12. Cut the animals out with the saw.

3. Beginning with the medium-grade sandpaper and finishing with the fine, sand all the surfaces of the animals. Also sand the pole.

4. Paint all sides and edges of the animals, pole, and pegs with the primer. Let all of the primed pieces dry. Then paint all the pieces with several coats of the white paint, letting the paint dry between coats.

5. Draw or trace the pattern details on both sides of each animal. For the cows, paint the outline and details with the black paint pen. Paint the spots with black paint. Paint the edges red. (See photo.) For the bunnies, paint the bodies pink. Paint the spots and edges green.

6. For the cowboy clothes tree, measure up the pole every 2″ and draw a line all the way around. To achieve a checkerboard look, paint every other section black as you move up 1 side of the pole. Paint the other 3 sides in the same way, alternating the beginning color. (See photo.)

For the bunny clothes tree, begin at the bottom of the pole and draw a line around 3 sides of the pole, angling the line up ¼″ on each succeeding side. When you come to the last side of the pole, angle the line down to connect with the beginning of the line. Measure up the pole every 2″ and draw lines parallel to the first. To achieve a striped look, paint every other stripe green. (See photo.)

7. Paint the round ends of the pegs red

for the cowboy clothes tree and pink for the bunny clothes tree.

Assembling the Clothes Tree

1. With a pencil, mark the 2 drilling positions on the back flat edge of each animal where shown on the pattern. Stand the animals up side by side to make sure the positions are perfectly aligned with one another. Using the ⅜″ bit, drill 2 (1″-deep) holes in each animal at the marks.

2. Squeeze glue into the 2 holes in 1 animal and insert a dowel in each hole. Repeat for the other animals.

3. To attach the animals to the pole, mark corresponding holes in the 4 sides of 1 end of the pole. Make sure that the bottom edges of the animals are even with the bottom edge of the pole. Using the ⅜″ bit, drill 8 (½″-deep) holes in the pole.

4. Squeeze glue into each hole. Insert the dowels attached to the animals into the holes. Press the animals against the pole until they fit snugly against it. Let the glue dry.

5. To attach the 6 pegs at the top of the pole, make a mark 3″ from the top. On the same side of the pole, mark 8″ from the top. On the opposite side of the pole, make 2 marks to match those just made. Turn the pole to an unmarked side and mark 5″ from the top. On the opposite side of the pole make another mark to match. Using the ½″ bit, drill ½″-deep holes at a slight downward angle where marked.

6. Squeeze a small amount of glue into each hole and insert the pegs. Twist the pegs until they are tight. Let the glue dry. Touch up paint as needed.

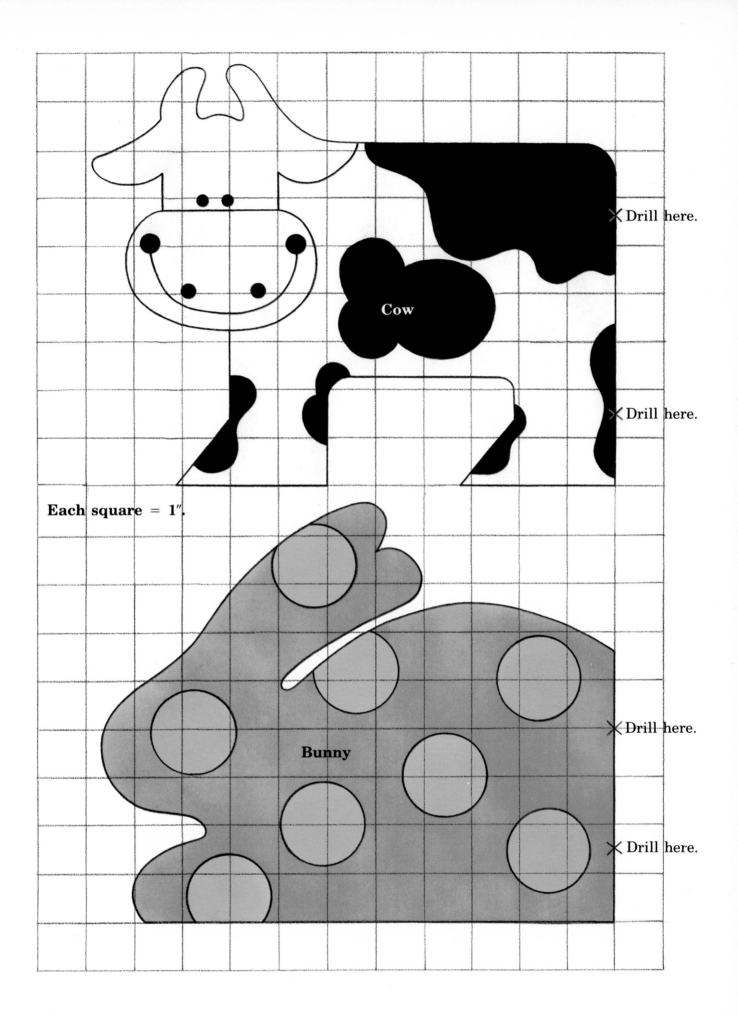

Cow

Drill here.

Drill here.

Each square = 1″.

Bunny

Drill here.

Drill here.

Cat & Mouse Pull Toy

Kids can create their own game of cat and mouse with this brightly colored pull toy. The spinning wheels will keep little feet coming and going.

You will need:
Tracing paper
1 (12″-long) pine 1 x 6
1 (26″-long) pine 1 x 4
Jigsaw
Hand saw
Electric drill with ¼″, ⅛″, ⅜″, ⁷⁄₆₄″ bits
Sandpaper: medium, fine
Ruler
Acrylic paints: yellow, blue, turquoise, orange, pink, black
Paintbrushes
Clear acrylic enamel
Scraps of suede leather: blue, pink
Glue
2 (¼″-long) #2 flat-head wood screws
3 (1½″-long) #6 flat-head wood screws
4 (1¾″-long) #4 round-head wood screws
Flat-head screwdrivers: small, medium
45″ (¼″) green nylon cord
1 (1¼″-diameter) wooden bead
18″ (⅜″) blue nylon cord
Liquid ravel preventer
24 (¼″) washers
⅞ yard (½″-wide) blue ribbon
Brass bell

Figure B   Front

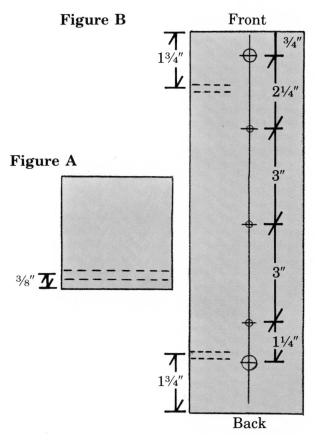

Figure A

Back

along the bottom, transfer the mouse pattern and markings to the wood. Use the jigsaw to cut out the mouse.

5. Sand all the pieces, using the medium sandpaper.

6. To attach the cord and the cat to the platform, you will need to drill 5 holes of varying diameters down the center of the platform. (Figure B.) Use the ruler to draw a line down the center. On the line, measure ¾″ from 1 end of the platform and drill a ¼″ hole. (This will be the front of the platform.) Measure 2¼″ from the first hole and drill a ⅛″ hole. Measure 3″ from the second hole and drill another ⅛″ hole. Measure 3″ from the third hole and drill another ⅛″ hole. Measure 1¼″ from the last hole and drill a ⅜″ hole.

1. Trace and cut out the patterns.

2. Trace around the cat pattern on the 1 x 6. Trace 4 wheels on the 1 x 4. Cut out all the shapes using the jigsaw.

3. From the remaining 1 x 4, use the hand saw to cut a 12″ length for the platform. Use the rest for the mouse.

4. Drill a ¼″ hole through the entire length of the mouse piece ⅜″ from the bottom edge. (Figure A.) With the hole

7. For the wheels, mark 2 holes on 1 long edge of the platform, positioning the marks 1¾" from the front and 1¾" from the back of the platform. (Figure B.) Repeat for the other side. Drill ⁷⁄₆₄" (1"-deep) holes at each mark. Also drill a ⅛" hole through the center of each wheel.

8. Paint the cat yellow, the platform blue, and the mouse, wheels, and pull bead turquoise. Let them dry. Sand the pieces lightly with the fine sandpaper and paint again. Let them dry. Transfer the stripes and facial features to the cat. Paint the stripes orange. Paint the mouth, cheeks, and inner ear pink. Paint the eyes and nose black. Paint black eyes on the mouse. Let them dry.

9. Paint all the pieces with several coats of clear enamel, allowing the enamel to dry between coats.

10. For the mouse, cut 4 outer ears from the blue suede and 2 inner ears from the pink suede. To make 1 ear, glue 2 outer ears together. Glue 1 inner ear to the center of the outer ear. Repeat for the second ear. Using the ¼" flat-head screw, screw 1 ear to the mouse where indicated on the pattern. To cover the screws, fold the ear in half at the bottom and glue it over the screw. Attach the other ear the same way.

Assembling the Pull Toy

1. To attach the cat to the platform, center the cat on the platform, with the back of the cat just in front of the back hole. Using the 1½" flat-head screws, screw the bottom of the cat to the platform beginning with the center ⅛" hole. Screw in the remaining 2 screws.

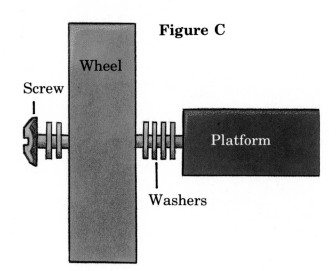

Figure C

2. For the pull cord, knot 1 end of the green cord. Bringing the cord up from underneath the platform, thread the unknotted end of the cord through the front hole. Make a second knot in the cord just above the hole. Thread the mouse and then the bead onto the cord. Knot the end of the cord.

For the tail, knot 1 end of the blue cord. Bringing the cord up from underneath the platform, thread the unknotted end through the back hole. Knot the end of the cord. Apply liquid ravel preventer to the ends of the cords to prevent them from raveling.

3. To attach the wheels, use the round-head screws to screw the wheels to the edges of the platform, placing 2 washers between each head of the screw and the wheel and 4 between each wheel and the platform. (Figure C.) Leave the screws loose enough for the wheels to turn easily. Paint the heads of the screws black.

4. Thread the ribbon through the bell and tie it in a bow around the cat's neck.

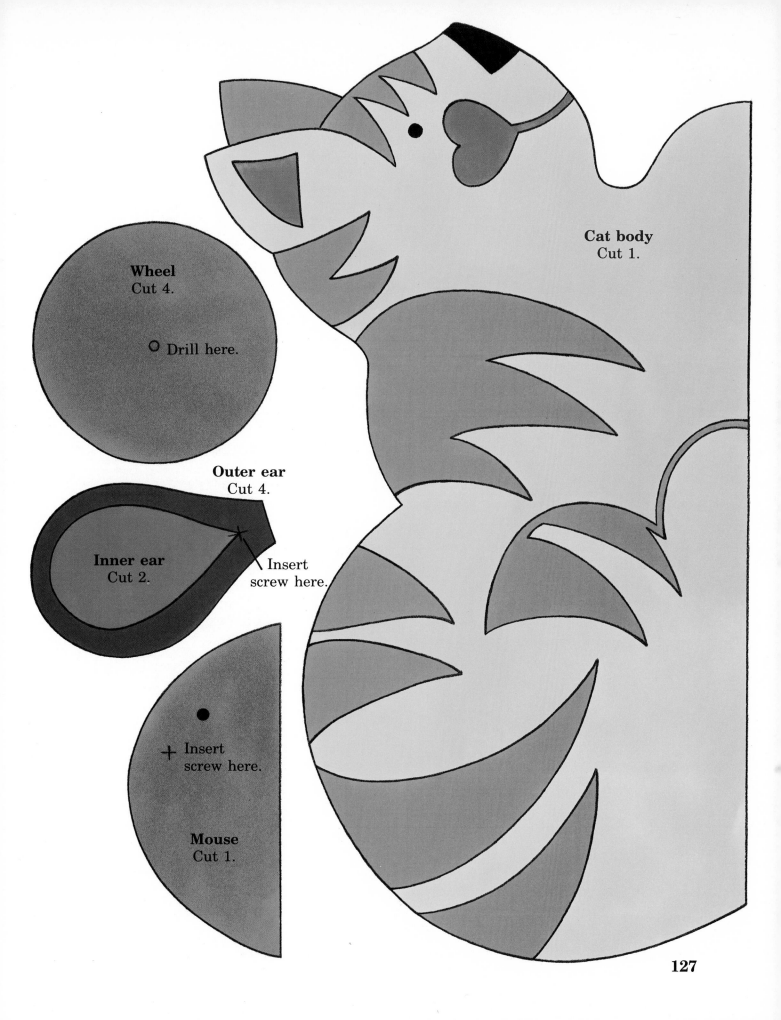

Wheel
Cut 4.

O Drill here.

Cat body
Cut 1.

Outer ear
Cut 4.

Inner ear
Cut 2.

Insert
screw here.

Insert
screw here.

Mouse
Cut 1.

127

Playhouse

Is it a summer cottage, a secret hideaway, a grand hotel? Your child can decide, as she spends hours in creative play made possible with felt, a card table, and a little sewing.

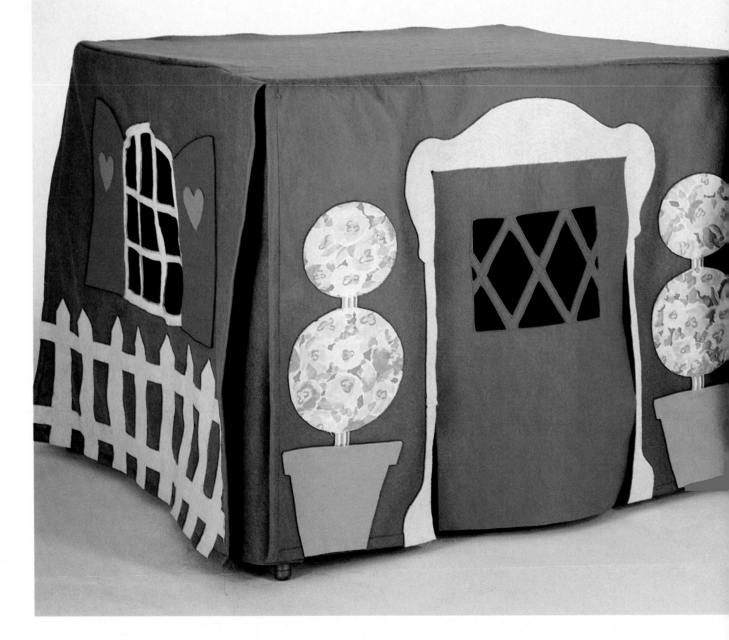

You will need:
3 yards (72″-wide) turquoise felt
Fabric marker
Tracing paper
1 yard (72″-wide) white felt
Fabric glue
⅔ yard (72″-wide) magenta felt
Scraps of lavender felt
2 (7″ x 8″) squares of peach felt
¼ yard of floral print polished cotton
18″ (⅞″-wide) ribbon

1. Use your card table as a guide for cutting out the pieces for the playhouse. To make the top of the playhouse, measure the top of the table. Add a ⅝″ seam allowance to all 4 sides and cut the top from the turquoise felt. Set the top aside.

2. To figure the side panel measurements, use 1 side of the table for the width. For the length, measure the distance from the top of the table to ½″ from the floor. Add a ⅝″ seam allowance to all 4 sides. Cut 4 panels from the turquoise felt. For the corner flaps, cut 4 pieces, each 12″ wide by the length of the side panels.

3. Turn under the seam allowance on 2 short sides and 1 long side of each panel piece and hem.

4. Enlarge the patterns as indicated. Transfer the patterns and markings to the tracing paper and cut out.

5. From the white felt, cut 3 (8-picket) fence sections. Using the photograph as a placement guide, glue the fence sections to the long hemmed edge of 3 side panels. (These will be the sides and back of the playhouse.) Set the remaining side panel aside.

129

6. Trace the window pattern 4 times onto the white felt. Transfer all stitching and cutting lines to the white felt and cut out the windows along the outside edges only.

7. Center 1 window on the right side of 1 side panel, with the bottom of the window 11″ from the bottom of the panel. Stitch the window in place on the outside stitching line only. Cut away the turquoise felt behind the window, being careful not to cut into the white felt of the window. On the wrong side of the panel, place another window behind the first, aligning edges and sandwiching the edges of the turquoise felt between. Stitch the windows together, stitching on all stitching lines. (See pattern.) Following the cutting lines, cut out the window panes, cutting through both layers of the white felt. Repeat for a second window on another panel.

8. Cut 8 shutters from the magenta felt. To make the shutters a double thickness, glue the back of 1 shutter to another shutter. Glue the doubled shutter in place on 1 side of a window. (See photo.) Repeat for the other 3 shutters.

9. Cut 4 hearts from the lavender felt. Glue each heart to a shutter, as indicated on the pattern.

10. To make the door opening, center the door pattern (not the door trim) along the remaining turquoise panel, aligning the bottom edges. Trace around the pattern and cut it out. Add a ⅝″ seam allowance along the top of the door pattern; then cut 2 doors from magenta felt. Transfer the markings for the window panes but don't cut the panes out yet.

11. To make the door a double thickness, place the 2 doors in the door opening, aligning the side and bottom edges. At the top edge, sandwich the turquoise felt of the front panel between the seam allowances of the 2 door pieces. Topstitch across the top of the door through all 3 layers. Glue the doors together.

12. Topstitch along the stitching lines of the door's window panes. Then cut them out as marked, cutting through both layers of felt.

13. Cut out the door trim from the white felt. Glue it in place around the door opening, covering the stitched edge at the top of the door and aligning the inside edges with the door opening. (See photo.)

14. To make the topiaries, cut 2 pots from the peach felt. From the floral print, cut 2 (7″) circles and 2 (5½″) circles. Cut the ribbon in half. Using the photograph as a guide, place 1 pot next to the door trim, aligning the bottom of the pot with the bottom of the front panel. For the trunk, center 1 end of the ribbon underneath the top edge of the pot. Glue the ribbon in place. Glue the pot in place. Center and glue the large circle on the ribbon, 1″ above the top edge of the pot. Center and glue the small circle ½″ above the large circle, covering the other end of the ribbon. Repeat for the other topiary.

15. To assemble the house, sew the panels to the top of the house 1 at a time, with right sides facing, using a ⅝″ seam and rounding the corners.

16. To add the corner pieces, place 1 piece diagonally across the wrong side of 1 corner. (See Figure.) Using a ⅝″ seam, stitch, rounding the corner. Repeat for the other 3 corners. Clip corners and trim excess fabric. Place the playhouse over the card table.

Figure

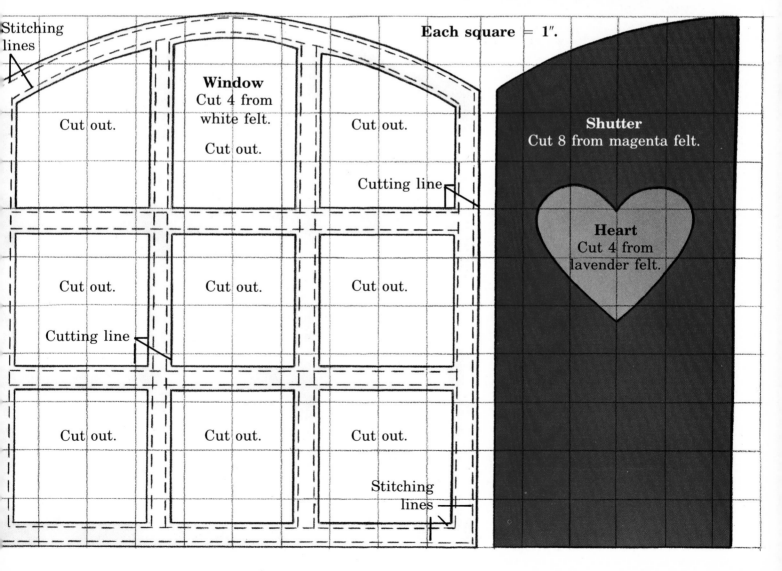

Stitching lines

Each square = 1″.

Cut out.

Window
Cut 4 from white felt.

Cut out.

Cut out.

Cutting line

Cut out.

Cut out.

Cut out.

Cutting line

Cut out.

Cut out.

Cut out.

Stitching lines

Shutter
Cut 8 from magenta felt.

Heart
Cut 4 from lavender felt.

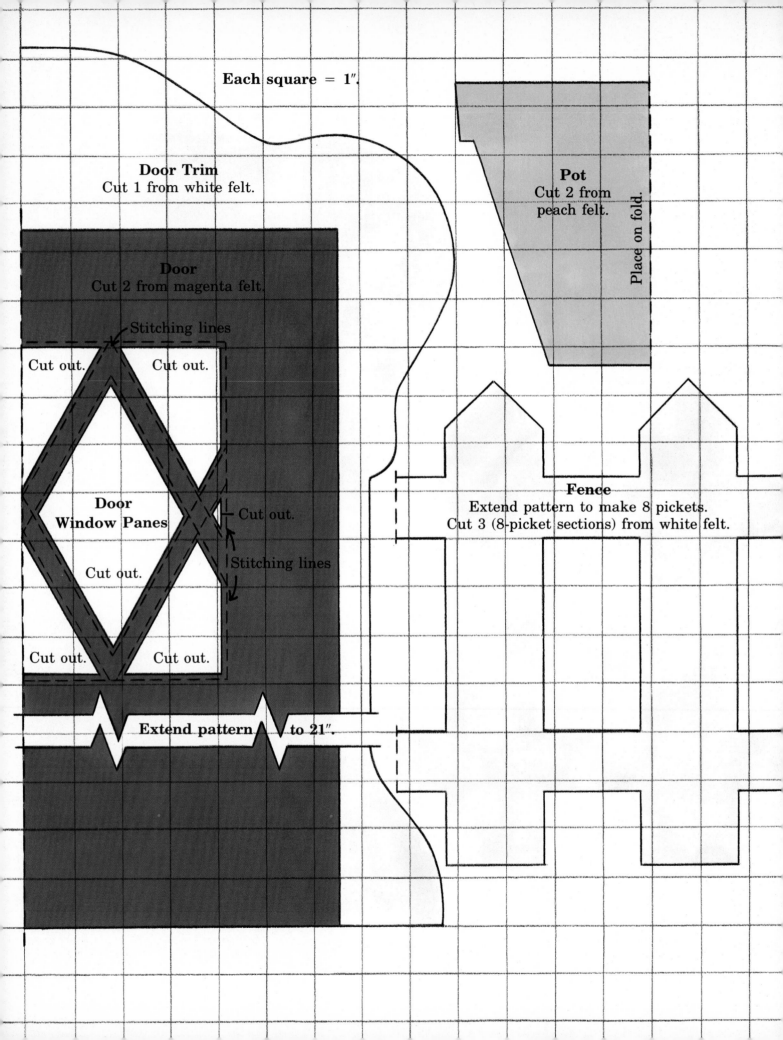

Each square = 1".

Door Trim
Cut 1 from white felt.

Pot
Cut 2 from
peach felt.

Place on fold.

Door
Cut 2 from magenta felt.

Stitching lines

Cut out.

Cut out.

**Door
Window Panes**

Cut out.

Cut out.

Cut out.

Cut out.

Cut out.

Stitching lines

Fence
Extend pattern to make 8 pickets.
Cut 3 (8-picket sections) from white felt.

Extend pattern to 21".

Clothespin Table & Chairs

With a few wooden clothespins and a little paint, you can create a rockin' good time for a favorite little girl and her doll. Spring-type wooden clothespins taken apart are the "boards" for this doll furniture.

Figure A—Parts of a Clothespin

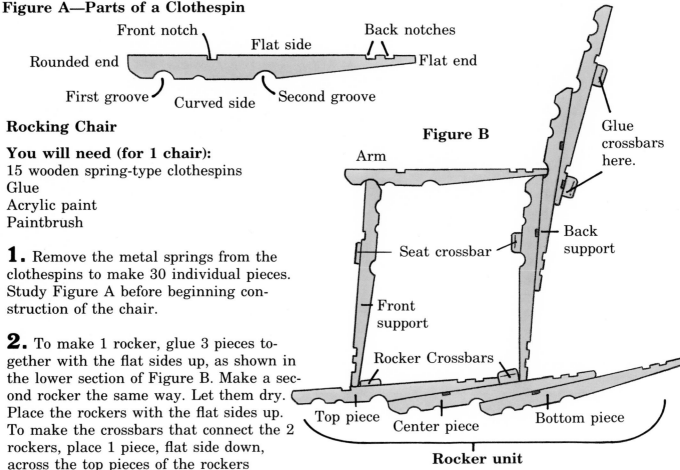

Figure A—Parts of a Clothespin

Front notch
Rounded end
Flat side
Back notches
Flat end
First groove
Curved side
Second groove

Figure B

Arm

Glue crossbars here.

Seat crossbar

Back support

Front support

Rocker Crossbars

Top piece
Center piece
Bottom piece

Rocker unit

Rocking Chair

You will need (for 1 chair):
15 wooden spring-type clothespins
Glue
Acrylic paint
Paintbrush

1. Remove the metal springs from the clothespins to make 30 individual pieces. Study Figure A before beginning construction of the chair.

2. To make 1 rocker, glue 3 pieces together with the flat sides up, as shown in the lower section of Figure B. Make a second rocker the same way. Let them dry. Place the rockers with the flat sides up. To make the crossbars that connect the 2 rockers, place 1 piece, flat side down, across the top pieces of the rockers slightly behind the first notches. Line up the ends of the crossbar with the outside edges of the rockers. Glue it in place. Place the second crossbar, flat side down, on top of the center pieces of the rockers, just behind the ends of the top pieces. (Figure B.) Glue it in place. Set the rocker unit aside.

3. Make the 2 supports for the chair back just as you made the rockers, except for the second crossbar. Glue the second crossbar, flat side down, across the ends of the top pieces. (Figure B.) Let them dry.

4. Place the chair back with the crossbars down. To finish the back of the chair, evenly space 4 pieces, rounded ends up and flat side down, across the cross-bars. (Figure C.) Glue the pieces in place and let them dry. Place a crossbar, flat side down, across the bottom support pieces, just above the lowest groove. (Figure C.) Glue it in place and let it dry.

5. For the front supports, place 2 pieces with the flat sides up. To connect the pieces, glue a crossbar, flat side down, just below the first notches in the pieces. (Figure B.) Let it dry.

Connect the front supports to the back with 2 pieces that will become the arms. With the flat side up, glue the flat end of 1 piece in the second groove of the center piece in the back support. (Figure B.) Glue the front support to the arm by placing the top end of the support piece in the first groove of the arm. Glue the second

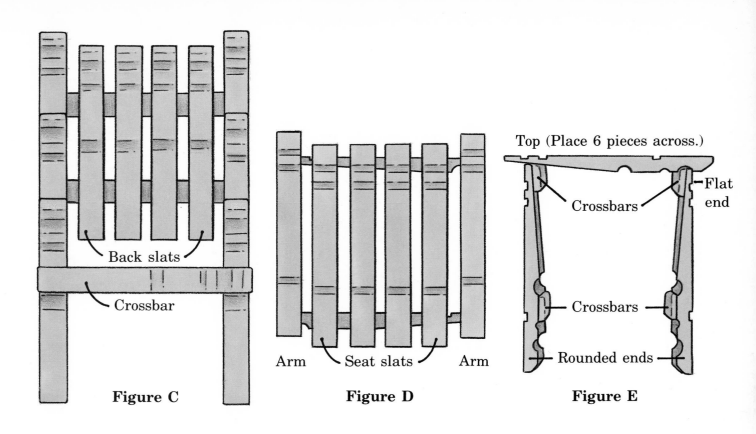

Figure C

Back slats

Crossbar

Figure D

Arm Seat slats Arm

Figure E

Top (Place 6 pieces across.)

Flat end

Crossbars

Crossbars

Rounded ends

arm on the other side of the chair in the same way. Let the glue dry.

6. For the seat, evenly space 4 pieces, flat side up, across the seat crossbars, placing the rounded ends of the pieces toward the front of the chair. (Figure D.) Glue them in place. Let the glue dry.

7. To connect the chair to the rocker unit, glue the front 2 supports to the front edge of the front crossbar of the rocker unit. Glue the back 2 supports to the back edge of the back crossbar. (Figure B.) Let the glue dry.

8. Paint the chair as desired using acrylic paint.

Table

You will need:
7 wooden spring-type clothespins
Glue
Acrylic paint
Paintbrush

1. Remove the metal springs from the clothespins to make 14 individual pieces. Study Figure A before beginning construction of the table.

2. For the table legs, place 2 pieces with the flat sides down. To make the crossbars that connect the legs, place another piece, flat side down, across the flat ends of the 2 legs. Line up the ends of the crossbar with the outside edges of the legs. Glue another crossbar about 1″ from the round ends of the legs. (Figure E.) Make another pair of legs the same way. Let the glue dry.

3. To make the top of the table, prop the legs so that the round ends of the legs are at the bottom and the crossbars are facing each other. Evenly space 6 pieces, flat side up, across the crossbars and glue them in place. (Figure E.) Let the glue dry.

4. Paint the table as desired, using acrylic paint.

Child's Picnic Set

Create the perfect mood for your child's afternoon tea or make-believe party with this child-size picnic table and bench ensemble. Made from simple cuts of wood, the completed pieces neatly fold for easy storage.

You will need (for the set):

Ruler
Tape measure
4 (8-foot) pine 1 x 6s
Table saw or hand-held power saw
Saber saw or coping saw
Electric drill with ⅝″ and ¼″ bits
Sandpaper
Wood glue
Hammer
4d finishing nails
Nailset
Wood filler
Socket wrench or needle-nose pliers
Latex paint
Paintbrushes
Water sealer (if the set will be used
   outside)

For the table:

6 (¼″ x 1″) bolts
12 (¼″) washers

For 2 benches:

12 (¼″ x 1″) bolts
24 (¼″) washers

Note: Just a reminder that little fingers could be pinched if children try to fold or unfold the table and benches. We recommend that this be a task for Mom or Dad.

Making the Table

1. Lay out the wood and mark the cutting lines as shown in Figure A. Also label the individual pieces. With the power saw, make the cross cuts. Then make the linear cuts. Divide the pieces into 2 stacks: 1 for the benches and 1 for the table.

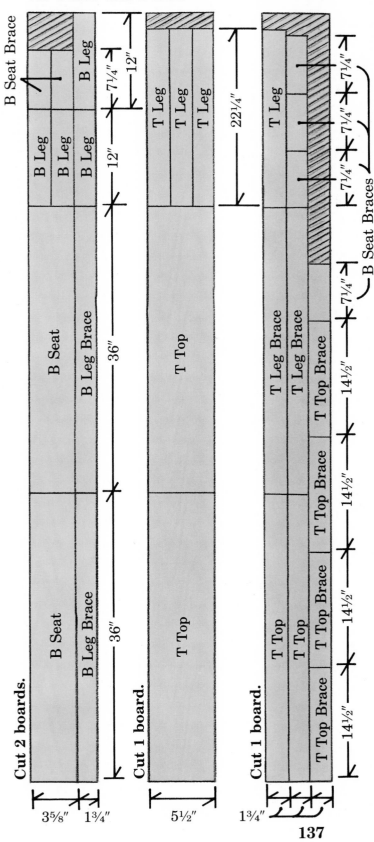

Figure A—Cutting Layout for Table and Bench

B = Bench
T = Table

137

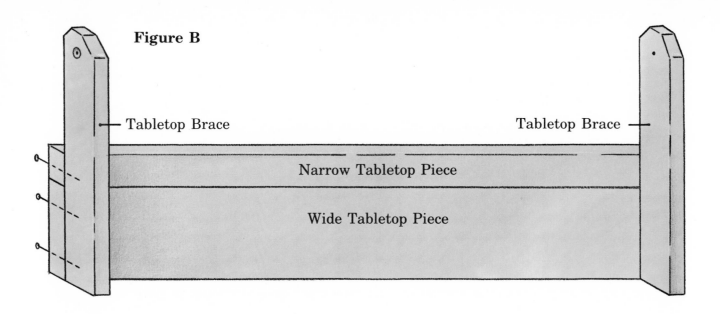

Figure B

Tabletop Brace

Tabletop Brace

Narrow Tabletop Piece

Wide Tabletop Piece

2. With the saber saw, round off 1 end of each leg and 1 end of each of the tabletop braces. Do not cut the angles for the leg bottom yet.

3. For the bolt placement on the tabletop braces, make a mark in the center of each brace about $\frac{7}{8}''$ from the rounded end. At each mark, use the $\frac{5}{8}''$ bit and drill a $\frac{3}{8}''$-deep countersink hole or a hole deep enough to clear the bolt head. With the $\frac{1}{4}''$ drill bit, drill all the way through the center of each hole.

4. For the bolt placement on the table legs, mark $\frac{7}{8}''$ from the rounded end of each of the 4 legs. Then turn the legs over and mark 11″ from the rounded end. Drill at each mark as you did for the tabletop braces, using first the $\frac{5}{8}''$ bit and then the $\frac{1}{4}''$ bit.

5. Trace the leg bottom pattern and cut it out. Lay the legs side by side with the $\frac{1}{4}''$ holes at the rounded ends facing up. Lay the pattern on 1 leg and trace the bottom angle. Repeat on the next leg. Flip the pattern and then trace it on the remaining 2 legs.

6. Sand all the pieces.

7. For $\frac{1}{2}$ of the tabletop, align the long edges of 1 wide tabletop piece and 1 narrow tabletop piece. (Figure B.) Treating these 2 pieces as 1, glue a tabletop brace across 1 end with the countersink hole to the outside. Glue another brace at the opposite end. For the other $\frac{1}{2}$ of the tabletop, align the remaining 2 tabletop pieces. This time measure $2\frac{1}{2}''$ from 1 end and glue a tabletop brace with the countersink hole to the inside. Glue the fourth brace $2\frac{1}{2}''$ from the opposite end. Let the glue dry.

Nail the tabletop pieces to the braces. Sink the nails using the nailset. Fill the holes with wood filler. Then sand the tabletop pieces again.

8. Position 2 legs so that the countersink holes at the top are facing. Glue a brace across the bottom as shown, extending the brace $\frac{3}{4}''$ beyond each leg. (Figure C.) Place the remaining legs so that the $\frac{1}{4}''$ holes at the top are facing. Glue a brace across the bottom, but this time extend the brace $1\frac{1}{2}''$ beyond each leg. Nail the braces in place. Sink the nails and fill the holes with wood filler. Sand the pieces again.

9. To see if the table will fold and unfold properly, assemble the pieces. (Figure D.) Stack 1 tabletop section on 1 leg section, matching ¼" holes. Insert 1 bolt through the tabletop brace. Next, slip on 1 washer. (This will be between the tabletop brace and the leg.) Now slip the bolt through the leg and add another washer; then add the nut. Use the socket wrench or needle-nose pliers to tighten the bolt and nut, keeping them loose enough for the legs to fold easily. Bolt the other leg and tabletop section together the same way. To join the 2 sections, bolt the legs together in the same way.

10. Disassemble the table and make any needed adjustments. Sand the parts again. While the table is disassembled, paint the parts as desired; apply the water sealant if the set will be used outdoors. Let the pieces dry at least 24 hours so that they won't stick together when they are reassembled. As you put the parts back together, put a drop of paint on the bolt threads just before you put on the nut. This will help to secure the bolt.

Making the Benches

1. To make the benches, repeat steps 2 and 3 of the table instructions.

2. For bolt placement in the legs, mark ⅞" from the rounded end of each leg. Then turn the legs to the other side and mark 4½" from the rounded end as you did for the table legs. Drill the holes at each mark as you did the table legs.

3. Sand all the pieces.

4. Glue 1 seat brace across the end of 1 piece of the seat as you did the tabletop brace. (Figure B.) Glue another brace on the opposite end of the same piece. On the other piece of the seat, glue 1 brace 2½" from 1 end of the seat. Glue the second brace 2½" from the opposite end. Let the glue dry. Repeat for the second bench.

Using 3 nails on each end, nail the seats to the braces. Sink the nails and fill the holes with wood filler. Then sand the seats again.

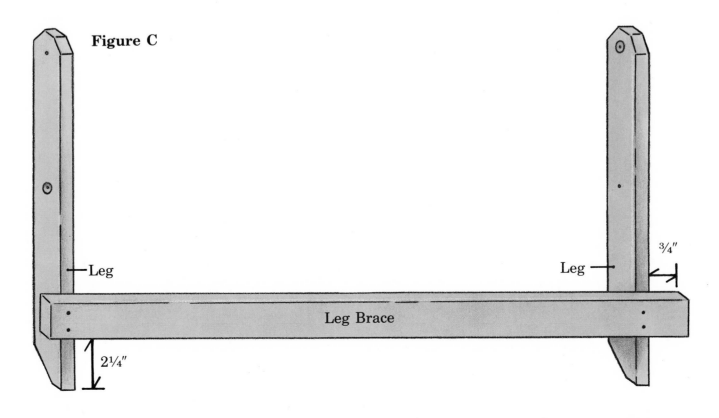

Figure C

Leg

Leg

¾"

Leg Brace

2¼"

Figure D

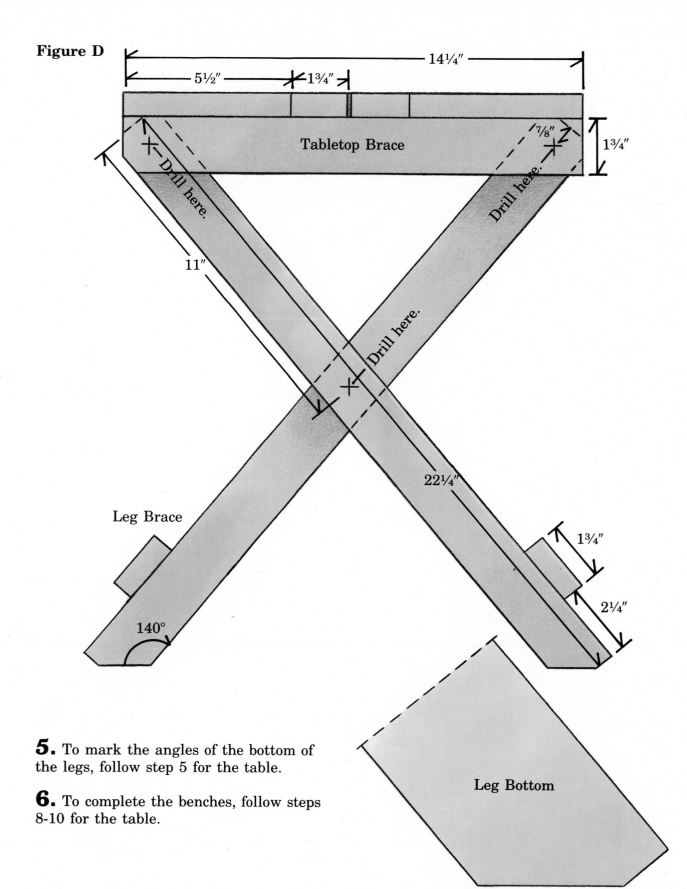

5. To mark the angles of the bottom of the legs, follow step 5 for the table.

6. To complete the benches, follow steps 8-10 for the table.

Sign-a-saur

This brightly colored dinosaur is a perfect way to mark special occasions such as birthday parties, slumber parties, or even a trip to camp. Always ready to go, he even carries his own pen! This friendly fellow, a modern version of an autograph book, will bring hours of fun to kids of all ages.

141

You will need:
Tracing paper
½ yard of lightweight orange cotton fabric
Scraps of fabric: pink, green, yellow
⅛ yard of fusible interfacing
Polyester stuffing
White acrylic paint
Small paintbrush
Black laundry marker
Acrylic yarn: yellow, orange, pink
1 (2½" x 5") piece of cardboard
Ballpoint pen

1. Enlarge the patterns as indicated. Transfer the patterns and markings to the tracing paper. Cut out the patterns.

2. Cut the patterns from the fabrics as indicated. For the spikes, cut 4 from each color of fabric, for a total of 16 spikes. For the feet, cut 8 from the green fabric and 4 from the interfacing.

3. With right sides facing and raw edges aligned, stitch 2 same-color spikes together, leaving the straight edge open as indicated on the pattern. Clip the curves and turn. Make the other 15 spikes the same way.

   With 1 body piece right side up, position the spikes between A and B along the back seam line with raw edges aligned and points towards the center of the body. Edges of spikes should overlap slightly. Baste in place.

4. With right sides facing and raw edges aligned, pin the gusset and the body piece together, matching points C and D on the gusset with points C and D on the body. Stitch the pieces together.

5. For the loop, cut a 1" x 2" strip from the yellow fabric. Turn under each long edge ¼" and press. Fold in half lengthwise with wrong sides facing and press again. Machine-stitch this long edge

closed. Fold the strip in half to form a loop. With the loop pointing to the center of the body, align the raw edges of the loop with the right side of the body piece where indicated on the pattern. Baste the loop in place.

6. With right sides facing and raw edges aligned, stitch the body pieces together, stitching through all layers and catching the spikes and loop in the seam. Leave a 3" opening below the loop for turning. Trim the seams, clip the curves, turn, and press. Stuff the body firmly and slipstitch the opening closed.

7. Following the manufacturer's instructions, fuse 1 interfacing foot to the wrong side of 1 green foot. With right sides facing and raw edges aligned, stitch the interfaced foot to a non-interfaced foot, leaving an opening as indicated for turning. Trim the seams, clip the curves, and turn. Slipstitch the opening closed and press. Repeat to make 3 more feet. Slipstitch the feet to the bottom of the sign-a-saur. (See photo.)

8. With a pencil, draw an eye on each side of the face. Paint the inside of the eyes white. Let them dry. With the laundry marker, outline the eyes and eyelashes and fill in the pupil of each eye.

9. To make the hair, wrap 1 color of yarn around the cardboard about 40 to 50 times. Wrap the second color next to the first. Repeat for the remaining color. Slip a piece of yarn between the loops and the cardboard, and tie it very tightly. Remove the cardboard. With scissors, cut through the loops on the end opposite the tie. Trim the ends even and shape into a pom-pom. Stitch the pom-pom securely to the top of the sign-a-saur's head.

10. Place the pen in the loop.

142

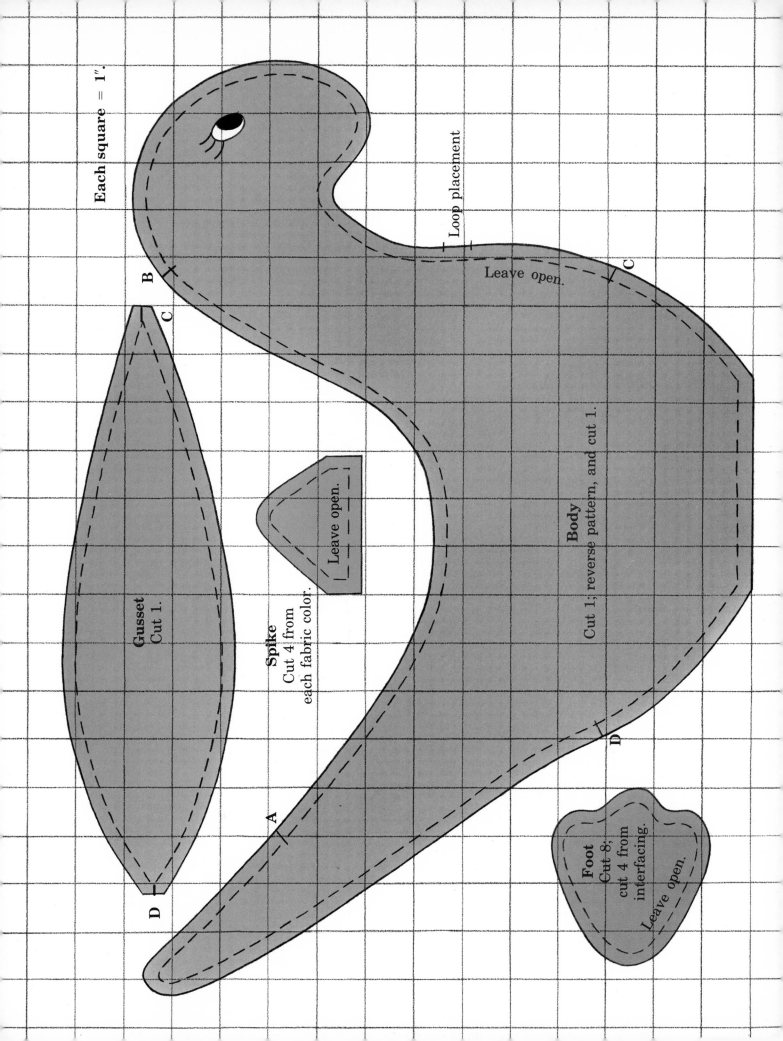

Each square = 1".

Loop placement

Leave open.

B

C

Leave open.

Gusset
Cut 1.

Spike
Cut 4 from
each fabric color.

Body
Cut 1; reverse pattern, and cut 1.

C

D

D

A

Foot
Cut 8;
cut 4 from interfacing.
Leave open.

Designers & Contributors

Barbara Ball, North Pole Village buildings, 27; Paper Dolls, 35.

Lowell Baltzell, Child's Picnic Set, 136.

Patricia Ramey Channell, Sign-a-saur, 141.

Alice London Cox, Bathtime Trio, 107; Party Purses, 118.

Kim Eidson Crane, Christmas Tree Banner, 42; Candy Cane Mice, 50; Button Covers, 98.

Connie Formby, North Pole Entrance, 24.

Frivols, Snowman Sweatshirt, 104.

Camie Pritchard Griffin, Argyle Sweater, 116.

Deborah Hastings, Nativity Shadow Puppets, 86; Playhouse, 128; Clothespin Table & Chairs, 133.

Linda Hendrickson, Santa Sack, 61; Pop-up Package Toppers, 66; Cinnamon Baskets, 84; Wild 'n Wooly Headbands, 110; Cat & Mouse Pull Toy, 124.

Allison Kearney and Lee Nix, Clothes Trees, 120.

Betsy Scott, Copycat Cards, 68; Team Tees, 114.

Linda Martin Stewart, Clothespin Angels, 52; Shadow Box Greetings, 70; Fruit Place Mats, 100.

Madeline O'Brien White, Santa & Reindeer Wraps, 54; Silly Pins, 79; Cigar Boxes, 82; Lace Doily Frames, 95.

Karen Ann Wiant, Origami Ornaments, 47.

John Willenbecher, Kitty Cottage, 74.

Special thanks to **Lowell Baltzell, Linda Keller and Barkley, Canterbury Day School,** and to the following shops in Birmingham, Alabama for sharing their resources: **Applause Dancewear & Accessories; Chocolate Soup, Inc.; Huffstutler's Hardware Home Center; Jack N' Jill Shop; Sikes Children's Shoes; Smith's Variety of Mountain Brook; Vestavia Hills Apothecary.**